SRA Spelling Mastery

Workbook

Level E

Robert Dixon
Siegfried Engelmann

Columbus, OH

The McGraw·Hill Companies

Cover Photo Credit: Getty Images, Inc.

Illustrations: Janice Skivington

SRAonline.com

Printed in the United States of America.

Send all inquiries to:
SRA/McGraw-Hill
4400 Easton Commons
Columbus, OH 43219

ISBN 0-07-604485-8

14 15 16 QLM 15 14

Lesson 1

A

thought   worth   match   use   power   reason

B

1. _____ mist
2. _____ misprint
3. _____ handle
4. _____ mishandle
5. _____ restless
6. _____ handleless

C

1. _____
2. _____
3. _____
4. _____
5. _____
6. _____

D

1. Some wild berries contane poison.   _____
2. Phisical exercise helps your body's development.   _____
3. Both sience and writing classes are featuring a
   panel of speakers.   _____

Lesson 2

A

doubt   mother   print   place   price   view

B

1. _____ power

2. _____ powerful

3. _____ thoughtful

4. _____ doubtless

5. _____ motherless

6. _____ misuse

C

1. _____

2. _____

3. _____

4. _____

5. _____

6. _____

D

1. The union of trucks formed a protetive wall. _____

2. There are many dutys as a science teacher. _____

3. He used logic to solve a magor crime. _____

Lesson 3

A

b u a k t m i s o r g e i f

B

cover   like   cure   move   fresh   serve

C

1. _____ reason   3. _____ coverless   5. _____ printable

2. _____ reasonable   4. _____ mother   6. _____ powerless

D

1. _____   3. _____

2. _____   4. _____

E

These words are in the puzzle.
Circle seven or more of the words.

brown	vein	lose
win	breathe	fault
spent	source	quick
many	swim	trend

b	s	s	v	w	t	f
q	r	s	p	v	r	a
u	l	o	s	e	e	u
i	q	u	w	i	n	l
c	e	r	i	n	d	t
k	o	c	m	a	n	y
b	r	e	a	t	h	e

Lesson 4

A

sound   quote   guide   name   base   sore

B

1. _____ + _____ = reasonable

2. _____ + _____ + _____ = returnable

3. _____ + _____ = remove

4. _____ + _____ = worthless

5. _____ + _____ = misshape

6. _____ + _____ + _____ = resourceful

7. _____ + _____ = misquote

8. _____ + _____ = powerful

C

Make a small **v** above every vowel letter.
Make a small **c** above every consonant letter.

n   e   i   f   o   b   u   c   t   p   a   d   h   i   m   e   o

D

Cross out the misspelled words in these sentences.
Then write the words correctly above the crossed-out words.

Meny people where late.

Maby thay need sum help.

E

These words are in the puzzle.
Circle seven or more of the words.

replace	hope	sneak
niece	note	length
sleeve	leave	listen
last	little	fence

b	l	i	s	t	e	n
c	l	i	h	n	r	m
l	a	s	t	o	e	s
e	l	n	r	t	p	l
n	z	e	i	e	l	e
g	r	a	a	e	a	e
t	i	k	e	v	c	v
h	f	e	n	c	e	e

F

Each sentence has one misspelled word.
Write each word correctly on the blank.

1. I hope you retain your pashion for science.   _____

2. She was regresing instead of getting better.   _____

3. Playing lojic games makes me tense.   _____

Lesson 5 is a test lesson.
There is no worksheet.

Lesson 6

A

1. _____
2. _____
3. _____
4. _____

5. _____
6. _____
7. _____
8. _____

B

1. like + able = _____
2. like + ness = _____
3. cheer + ful = _____
4. price + less = _____
5. guide + ing = _____
6. hope + ing = _____
7. hope + less = _____
8. quote + able = _____

C

Fill in the blanks to show the morphographs in each word.

1. _____ + _____ = powerful
2. _____ + _____ = reserve
3. _____ + _____ + _____ = remarkable
4. _____ + _____ + _____ = helplessness
5. _____ + _____ + _____ = painfulness
6. _____ + _____ = report

D

Cross out the misspelled words in these sentences.
Then write the words correctly above the crossed-out words.

I thougth they were helples.

We found a plase with a restfull view.

Lesson 7

A

breath   fashion   fair   solve   source   tribe

B

1. stage + ing = _____
2. time + less = _____
3. cure + able = _____
4. firm + ness = _____
5. serve + ing = _____
6. use + less = _____
7. fear + ful = _____
8. trace + ed = _____

C

Nineteen athletes exercised throughout the morning.

_____

_____

D

1. _____   4. _____

2. _____   5. _____

3. _____   6. _____

E

Fill in the blanks to show the morphographs in each word.

1. _____ + _____ = resource

2. _____ + _____ + _____ = helplessness

3. _____ + _____ + _____ = returning

4. _____ + _____ = faithful

5. _____ + _____ + _____ = refillable

6. _____ + _____ + _____ = youthfulness

Lesson 8

_ _ _ e _ _ _ _ _ _ h l e _ e _

_ x _ _ c _ s _ _ _ _ _ o u _ _ _ _ _

_ _ _ _ o _ _ i _ _.

_____

_____

B

1. grab	**4.** move	**7.** art	**10.** plan
2. reason	**5.** drip	**8.** water	**11.** run
3. win	**6.** star	**9.** slip	**12.** poison

C

Add the morphographs together.
Some of the words follow the rule about dropping the final **e**.

1. name + ed = _____

2. solve + ing = _____

3. sore + ness = _____

4. guide + ed = _____

5. fashion + able = _____

6. price + ing = _____

7. price + less = _____

8. use + ful = _____

9. re + place + ing = _____

10. use + ed = _____

D

Write the correct word for each sentence.

1. Did you **here/hear** me?

   _____

2. Please put these over **there/their.**

   _____

3. Thank you **vary/very** much.

   _____

4. The cat is licking its **tale/tail.**

   _____

5. There is a **hole/whole** in my shoe.

   _____

6. Will you **loan/lone** me some money?

   _____

7. That answer is **write/right.**

   _____

8. I'm chewing a **peace/piece** of gum.

   _____

E

Fill in the blanks to show the morophographs in each word.

1. _____ + _____ = recover

2. _____ + _____ + _____ = refreshing

3. _____ + _____ = fairness

4. _____ + _____ + _____ = painfulness

5. _____ + _____ + _____ = misspelling

6. _____ + _____ = workable

F

Each sentence has one misspelled word.
Write each word correctly on the blank.

1. The vase is brakeable, so handle it carefully.   _____

2. I doubt if the cure is as painfull as the disease.   _____

3. Mother likes to quote reasenable advice from others.   _____

Lesson 9

A

rich   globe   sign   value   store   scribe

B

_ _ _ _ _ _ _ _ _ _ _ _ _ _ _ _ _ _ _

_ _ _ _ _ _ _ _ _ _ _ _ _ _ _ _ _ _ _

_ _ _ _ _ _ _ _ _.

_____

_____

C

1. _____   4. _____

2. _____   5. _____

3. _____   6. _____

D

1. wonder   3. drip   5. skin   7. cover   9. trip   11. brother

2. best   4. big   6. kind   8. scar   10. mad   12. hop

E

Add these morphographs together.
Some of the words follow the rule about dropping the final **e.**

1. value + able   = _____

2. solve + ing   = _____

3. re + source + ful = _____

4. un + fair + ness = _____

5. shame + less   = _____

6. like + ed   = _____

7. have + ing   = _____

F

Write the correct word for each sentence. If you're not sure
of a word, look it up in the list of homonyms on pages 196–198.

1. My **feat/feet** itch.   _____

2. Most countries want **peace/piece.**   _____

3. Do you like this **weather/whether?**   _____

4. This desk is made from **wood/would.**   _____

5. Our room is **to/too** cold.   _____

6. We passed **threw/through** the tunnel.   _____

G

Each sentence has one misspelled word.
Write each word correctly on the blank.

1. Mary is doubtfull about returning as a guide next year. _____

2. I thought the shirt was returnible because the price _____
was still on it.

3. Move the fresh flowers to a safer plase.   _____

Lesson 10 is a test lesson.
There is no worksheet.

Lesson 11

A

1. _____

   _____

2. _____

   _____

B

length   strength   fright   tough   short   loose

C

1. stop + ing   = _____

2. sad + ness   = _____

3. reason + ing = _____

4. plan + ed   = _____

5. hop + ing   = _____

6. star + less = _____

7. snug + ness = _____

8. pain + ful   = _____

D

valuable	replace	reason	helplessness
fashion	guide	scribe	breathless
thoughtful	powerless	solving	signal

Add the morphographs together.
Some of the words follow the rule about dropping the final **e.**

1. serve + ing = _____

2. store + ed   = _____

3. hope + ful   = _____

4. hope + ing   = _____

5. smile + ing = _____

6. ripe + est   = _____

7. doubt + less = _____

8. prove + ing = _____

Each sentence has one misspelled word.
Write each word correctly on the blank.

1. It would be pointless to hire him if he misspells and   _____
   missfiles things.

2. A portable radio still needs power to make sownd.   _____

3. My back is soar from having a sleepless night.   _____

Lesson 12

CVC + V

1. trap + ed = _____
2. big + est = _____
3. spot + less = _____
4. wonder + ful = _____
5. slip + ed = _____
6. step + ing = _____
7. mother + ing = _____
8. sad + est = _____

B

Cross out the misspelled words in these sentences.
Then write the words correctly above the crossed-out words.

The juge was resonable and fare.

Someone plased a sine on the stor.

C

These words are in the puzzle.
Circle nine or more of the words.

choicest	bridge	loose
live	read	break
house	solve	shops
greatest	pool	tent
seek	ruling	

c	b	r	i	d	g	e	g
s	h	b	r	e	a	k	r
p	o	o	l	o	o	s	e
r	u	l	i	n	g	h	a
r	s	s	v	c	t	o	t
e	e	e	e	e	e	p	e
c	h	a	e	o	n	s	s
p	o	o	d	k	t	t	t

Lesson 13

A

People weren't interested in the photograph.

_____

_____

B

1. _____

_____

2. _____

_____

C

1. wander + ing = _____
2. snap + ed = _____
3. swim + er = _____
4. flat + ness = _____
5. win + er = _____
6. step + ed = _____
7. great + est = _____
8. skid + ing = _____

D

Circle the misspelled word in each group.
Then write it correctly on the line.

1. powerful	2. hopefull	3. uncover	4. morning
signal	source	scribe	breth
shoper	place	formal	unfair
review	restless	fashun	globe

_____ _____ _____ _____

E

Add the morphographs together.

1. tribe + al   = _____

2. fine + er   = _____

3. life + less   = _____

4. fine + al   = _____

5. cure + able = _____

6. time + less = _____

7. globe + al   = _____

8. rage + ing   = _____

F

Each sentence has one misspelled word.
Write each word correctly on the blank.

1. Be careful not to misquote her or missuse her name. _____

2. I like to surve in a tennis match. _____

Lesson 14

firm   script   verse   tone   part   frost

B

_ e o _ _ _ _   _ _ _ _ _ n ' _   _ _ _ e r _ _ _ _ _

_ _ _ _ _ _   p h _ _ o _ _ _ p _.

_____

_____

C

1. _____ + _____ = _____
2. _____ + _____ = _____
3. _____ + _____ = _____
4. _____ + _____ = _____
5. _____ + _____ = _____
6. _____ + _____ = _____

D

Circle the misspelled word in each group.
Then write it correctly on the line.

1. tough	2. greatest	3. useles	4. scribe
gide	fright	widest	valueable
helpless	lenght	sounded	resource
formal	unhappy	straining	reserve

_____   _____   _____   _____

Lesson 15 is a test lesson.
There is no worksheet.

Lesson 16

crease   shrink   change   press   claim   quest

B

‒ ‒ ‒ ‒ ‒ ‒   ‒ ‒ ‒ ‒ ‒ ‒ ‒   ‒ ‒ ‒ ‒ ‒ ‒ ‒

‒ ‒   ‒ ‒ ‒   ‒ ‒ ‒ ‒ ‒ ‒ ‒ ‒ ‒ ‒ .

_____

_____

C

1. _____   4. _____

2. _____   5. _____

3. _____   6. _____

D

Add the morphographs together.
Some of the words follow the final-**e** rule.

1. peace + ful   = _____

2. hope + less   = _____

3. take + ing   = _____

4. fine + al   = _____

5. re + fine + ed = _____

6. large + est   = _____

7. crease + ed   = _____

8. loose + en   = _____

9. lone + ly   = _____

10. hide + ing   = _____

Lesson 17

A

strict   create   tense   state   treat   govern

B

1. _____

_____

2. _____

_____

C

1. happy + ness = _____
2. try + ed   = _____
3. play + ful   = _____
4. pity + ful   = _____
5. carry + ing = _____
6. carry + ed = _____
7. say + ing   = _____
8. worry + er = _____

D

| ly | mad | ness | fine | ripe | er | est |

1. _____   6. _____
2. _____   7. _____
3. _____   8. _____
4. _____   9. _____
5. _____

Add the morphographs together.
Some of the words follow the final-**e** rule.
Some of them follow the doubling rule.

1. hope + ful = _____

2. hope + ing = _____

3. hop + ing = _____

4. globe + al = _____

5. de + fine + ing = _____

6. snug + est = _____

7. wonder + ful = _____

8. loose + ly = _____

9. sad + ness = _____

10. slip + ing = _____

11. un + re + solve + able = _____

12. mad + ly = _____

Each sentence has one misspelled word.
Write each word correctly on the blank.

1. Nineteen athleates raced through the streets. _____

2. How did you recover from that remarkable feet? _____

3. I was hopping to hear your report. _____

Lesson 18

A

1. _____   4. _____

2. _____   5. _____

3. _____   6. _____

B

Change **y** when consonant-and-**y** + anything except **i.**

Add the morphographs together.
Some of the words follow the rule about changing **y** to **i.**

1. sturdy + ness   = _____

2. dry + ing   = _____

3. carry + ed   = _____

4. fancy + est   = _____

5. play + ing   = _____

6. pity + ful   = _____

7. nasty + est   = _____

8. study + ing   = _____

C

Make nine real words from the morphographs in the box.

less	star	ing	hope	ed	use	spot

1. _____   6. _____

2. _____   7. _____

3. _____   8. _____

4. _____   9. _____

5. _____

D

Write the correct word for each sentence. If you're not sure
of a word, look it up in the list of homonyms on pages 196–198.

1. Fifteen minus seven is **ate/eight.** _____

2. **Meet/Meat** me after school. _____

3. **Wear/Where** are you going? _____

4. That was quite a **tail/tale** Sandy told. _____

5. The runners **vary/very** their speed. _____

6. Do the books go **their/there?** _____

7. Turn **right/write** at the sign. _____

8. I finished the **hole/whole** report. _____

E

Each sentence has one misspelled word.
Write each word correctly on the blank.

1. The weather will very across the globe. _____

2. You'll get used to the sorness in your feet. _____

3. If Jack excercized more, his restlessness would
   go away. _____

Lesson 19

A

Anybody would rather be healthy instead of rich.

_____

_____

B

1. _____ + _____ = _____

2. _____ + _____ = _____

3. _____ + _____ = _____

4. _____ + _____ = _____

5. _____ + _____ = _____

6. _____ + _____ = _____

C

1. _____

2. _____

3. _____

4. _____

5. _____

6. _____

7. _____

8. _____

D

Fill in the blanks to show the morphographs in each word.

1. _____ + _____ + _____ + _____ = unreformed

2. _____ + _____ + _____ = departed

3. _____ + _____ + _____ + _____ = misreported

4. _____ + _____ + _____ + _____ = unconfirmed

5. _____ + _____ + _____ = reinstate

6. _____ + _____ + _____ = helplessly

7. _____ + _____ + _____ = restfully

8. _____ + _____ = resource

9. _____ + _____ + _____ = frightening

10. _____ + _____ + _____ = uselessness

11. _____ + _____ + _____ = confronted

12. _____ + _____ + _____ = delights

E

Each sentence has one misspelled word.
Write each word correctly on the blank.

1. I liked reading the tail even with its misspellings. _____

2. The briteness of her smile makes her very likable. _____

3. This fashionable piece of furniture is timeles. _____

Lesson 20 is a test lesson.
There is no worksheet.

Lesson 21

_ _ _ _ o _ _ _ o _ _ _ _ _ _ _ _ _ _

_ e a _ _ _ _ _ _ _ e a _ _ _ _ _ _ _.

_____

_____

B

straight   found   settle   agree   claim

C

1. _____ + _____ = facing
2. _____ + _____ = running
3. _____ + _____ = happiness
4. _____ + _____ = swimmer
5. _____ + _____ = valuable
6. _____ + _____ + _____ = reserved
7. _____ + _____ = pitiful
8. _____ + _____ + _____ = exchanging

D

1. _____ + _____ = _____
2. _____ + _____ = _____
3. _____ + _____ = _____
4. _____ + _____ = _____
5. _____ + _____ = _____
6. _____ + _____ = _____

Cross out the misspelled words in these sentences.
Then write the words correctly above the crossed-out words.

Are you intrested in incresing your strenht?

There are ninteen people in the photegraph.

Each sentence has one misspelled word.
Write each word correctly on the blank.

1. The farmer was hopful that he would have the _____
   biggest peppers.

2. The saddest part of the skirpt is coming up soon. _____

3. The people in the photograph wernt smiling. _____

Lesson 22

A

_ _ _ _ _ _ _ _ _ _ _ _ _ _ _ _ _ _

_ _ _ _ _ _ _ _ _ _ _ _ _ _ _ _ _ _ .

B

| prove | cause | great | text | spirit | thirst |

C

Figure out the rules and write them.
Remember to spell the words correctly.

with anything except **i** . . . **i** in a word when the . . . the next morphograph

begins . . . change the **y** to . . . word ends consonant-and-**y** and

word when the next . . . final **e** from a . . . with **v** . . . drop the . . . morphograph

begins

D

1. win   **2.** low   **3.** swim   **4.** chew   **5.** draw

Add the morphographs together.
Some of the words follow the rule about changing **y** to **i**.

1. stray + ed = _____

2. cry + ing = _____

3. worry + ed = _____

4. nasty + er = _____

5. pity + ing = _____

6. deny + al = _____

7. try + al = _____

8. play + ful = _____

F

Fill in the blanks to show the morphographs in each word.
Remember to spell each morphograph correctly.

1. _____ + _____ = starring

2. _____ + _____ + _____ = reserved

3. _____ + _____ = final

4. _____ + _____ = happiest

5. _____ + _____ = sadden

6. _____ + _____ + _____ = resourceful

7. _____ + _____ + _____ = exchanging

8. _____ + _____ = lucky

Lesson 23

A

1. _____

_____

2. _____

_____

B

Write the correct spelling for each word.
Then write one of these letters after each number.

Write **O** if the word is spelled by just putting the morphographs together.
Write **A** if the final-**e** rule explains why the spelling is changed.
Write **B** if the doubling rule explains why the spelling is changed.
Write **C** if the **y**-to-**i** rule explains why the spelling is changed.

1. _____ vary + ed   = _____

2. _____ sad + ness   = _____

3. _____ tense + ion   = _____

4. _____ play + ful   = _____

5. _____ prove + en   = _____

6. _____ swim + er   = _____

7. _____ low + est   = _____

8. _____ pity + ful   = _____

9. _____ settle + ment = _____

10. _____ change + ing = _____

Add the morphographs together.

Remember: The morphograph **y** is a vowel letter.

1. rate + ion   = _____

2. treat + ment   = _____

3. con + text   = _____

4. re + in + state   = _____

5. edge + y   = _____

6. wreck + age   = _____

7. con + fine + ment = _____

8. ease + y   = _____

9. pro + claim + ed   = _____

10. in + crease + ing   = _____

Figure out the rules and write them.

word when the next morphograph . . . drop the final **e** from a . . .

begins with **v**

_____

_____

a short word when the . . . the next morphograph begins with **v** . . .

word ends **cvc** and . . . double the final **c** in

_____

_____

Lesson 24

A

1. _____

_____

2. _____

_____

B

1. _____   4. _____

2. _____   5. _____

3. _____   6. _____

C

1. _____   4. _____

2. _____   5. _____

3. _____

D

Write the correct spelling for each word.
Then write one of these letters after each number.

Write **O** if the word is spelled by just putting the morphographs together.
Write **A** if the final-**e** rule explains why the spelling is changed.
Write **B** if the doubling rule explains why the spelling is changed.
Write **C** if the **y**-to-**i** rule explains why the spelling is changed.

1. _____ poison + ed = _____

2. _____ hurry + ed = _____

3. _____ carry + ing = _____

4. _____ trap + er = _____

5. _____ happy + ness = _____

6. _____ ease + y = _____

7. _____ proud + ly = _____

8. _____ late + ly = _____

9. _____ tense + ion = _____

10. _____ clap + ing = _____

E

Each sentence has one misspelled word.
Write each word correctly on the blank.

1. I'd be surprised if anybody ate that meet.   _____

2. All of the reckage from the boats floated inland.   _____

3. Which rocks are you useing?   _____

Lesson 25 is a test lesson.
There is no worksheet.

34   Lesson 24

Lesson 26

Write the correct spelling for each word.
Then write one of these letters after each number.

Write **O** if the word is spelled by just putting the morphographs together.
Write **A** if the final-**e** rule explains why the spelling is changed.
Write **B** if the doubling rule explains why the spelling is changed.
Write **C** if the **y**-to-**i** rule explains why the spelling is changed.

1. _____ low + er   = _____

2. _____ snap + ed   = _____

3. _____ store + age   = _____

4. _____ edge + y   = _____

5. _____ slip + ing   = _____

6. _____ move + ment   = _____

7. _____ fit + ness   = _____

8. _____ flaw + ed   = _____

9. _____ note + ion   = _____

10. _____ play + ing   = _____

11. _____ run + y   = _____

12. _____ like + able   = _____

Circle the misspelled word in each group.
Then write it correctly on the line.

1. fashion

poison

strate

rather

_____

2. glory

pleaze

place

settle

_____

3. brother

wrong

carry

hopeing

_____

4. prove

cawse

hurried

agree

_____

5. crease

change

request

ninteen

_____

6. choice

sorce

strength

studying

_____

7. sturdyness

recover

serve

priceless

_____

8. swimmer

serving

pitiful

lowwer

_____

Fill in the blanks to show the morphographs in each word.

1. _____ + _____ + _____ = repressive

2. _____ + _____ + _____ = depression

3. _____ + _____ + _____ = expressed

4. _____ + _____ = feature

5. _____ + _____ + _____ = defeated

6. _____ + _____ = passion

7. _____ + _____ + _____ = profoundly

8. _____ + _____ + _____ = invaluable

Lesson 27

A

Write **s** or **es** in the second column.
Then add the morphographs together.

1. press   + _____ = _____

2. shop   + _____ = _____

3. buzz   + _____ = _____

4. box   + _____ = _____

5. stretch   + _____ = _____

6. rich   + _____ = _____

7. wash   + _____ = _____

8. script   + _____ = _____

B

1. _____

_____

2. _____

_____

C

1. _____   4. _____

2. _____   5. _____

3. _____

Write the correct word for each sentence.

1. The **weather/whether** has been great. _____

2. They found **their/there** things. _____

3. We **through/threw** rocks in the lake. _____

4. Pete ate **to/too** much. _____

5. Please bring those books **hear/here.** _____

6. I've never heard such a strange **tail/tale.** _____

Fill in the blanks to show the morophographs in each word.

1. _____ + _____ = poisonous

2. _____ + _____ = famous

3. _____ + _____ = relate

4. _____ + _____ + _____ = relative

5. _____ + _____ + _____ = reaction

6. _____ + _____ + _____ = expression

Each sentence has one misspelled word.
Write each word correctly on the blank.

1. The peaceful dogs became playfull when I began studying. _____

2. Todd tried to straighten up the storaje room. _____

3. She tried to press the crease out of the pakage. _____

Lesson 28

duty   danger   round   speak   fury   seize

B

1. _____
   _____

2. _____
   _____

C

1. _____   4. _____

2. _____   5. _____

3. _____

D

Write **s** or **es** in the second column.
Then add the morphographs together.

1. tax   + _____ = _____

2. brush + _____ = _____

3. claim + _____ = _____

4. waltz + _____ = _____

5. pass   + _____ = _____

6. light + _____ = _____

7. reach + _____ = _____

8. rich   + _____ = _____

Add the morphographs together.

1. deny + al = _____

2. glory + ous = _____

3. press + ure = _____

4. mis + con + cept + ion = _____

5. ex + cept + ion = _____

6. flaw + ed = _____

7. thirst + y = _____

8. ex + press + ion = _____

9. in + ject + ion = _____

10. seize + ure = _____

Each sentence has one misspelled word.
Write each word correctly on the blank.

1. You should darken the definning lines to create shadows. _____

2. You can make a helthy treat by drying some fruit. _____

3. She has remarkable skils, but she dresses poorly. _____

Lesson 29

A

1. _____   4. _____

2. _____   5. _____

3. _____

B

C

Make nine real words from the morphographs in the box.

est	mad	happy	ly	wide	ness	fine

1. _____   6. _____

2. _____   7. _____

3. _____   8. _____

4. _____   9. _____

5. _____

Fill in the blanks to show the morphographs in each word.

1. _____ + _____ + _____ = protective

2. _____ + _____ + _____ = injected

3. _____ + _____ + _____ = progressed

4. _____ + _____ + _____ = reception

5. _____ + _____ = texture

6. _____ + _____ + _____ = featuring

7. _____ + _____ = passion

8. _____ + _____ = studying

9. _____ + _____ = studious

10. _____ + _____ = signal

Each sentence has one misspelled word.
Write each word correctly on the blank.

1. I agree that we need a speedy settlement. _____

2. Latley I'm so hurried that I'm running around
   all the time. _____

3. The pressure of a courtroom triel worried her. _____

Lesson 30 is a test lesson.
There is no worksheet.

Lesson 31

A

The union of physical science and logic was a major development.

_____

_____

B

1. worry + _____ = _____
2. play + _____ = _____
3. try + _____ = _____
4. joy + _____ = _____
5. copy + _____ = _____
6. boy + _____ = _____
7. story + _____ = _____
8. study + _____ = _____
9. stay + _____ = _____
10. duty + _____ = _____

C

1. _____   4. _____
2. _____   5. _____
3. _____

Add the morphographs together.
Remember to use your spelling rules.

1. danger + ous   = _____

2. seize + ure   = _____

3. fury + ous   = _____

4. script + ure   = _____

5. quest + ion + able = _____

6. poison + ous   = _____

7. fur + y   = _____

8. please + ure   = _____

9. friend + ly + ness = _____

10. re + fuse + al   = _____

E

Cross out the misspelled words in these sentences.
Then write the words correctly above the crossed-out words.

Could you speak a little lowder, please?

Where are the fameous people?

Their was no reeson for the rejection.

Lesson 32

A

```
___  ___  ___  i o ___  ___  ___  ___  y s ___  ___  ___
___  ___  e ___  c ___  ___  ___  ___  o g ___  ___  ___
___  ___  j o ___  ___  ___  e ___  o ___  ___  ___  ___ .
```

_____

_____

B

1. _____   5. _____
2. _____   6. _____
3. _____   7. _____
4. _____   8. _____

C

Write **s** or **es** in the second column.
Then add the morphographs together.

1. boy   + _____ = _____
2. story + _____ = _____
3. try   + _____ = _____
4. worry + _____ = _____
5. baby + _____ = _____
6. fly   + _____ = _____
7. berry + _____ = _____
8. carry + _____ = _____

D

1. _____   4. _____

2. _____   5. _____

3. _____

E

These words are in the puzzle.
Circle seven or more of the words.

poison   found   photo

pound   concept   flat

lone   pity   whose

store   fact   proven

```
p   p   w   h   o   s   e   f
p   o   i   s   o   n   s   p
c   o   n   c   e   p   t   r
f   o   u   n   d   h   o   o
a   l   o   n   e   o   r   v
c   p   a   r   d   t   e   e
t   p   i   t   y   o   e   n
```

F

Each sentence has one misspelled word.
Write each word correctly on the blank.

1. She studied the statement and then changed   _____
   her mind.

2. He explained how to turn on the lights in the   _____
   building.

3. The treatment has been proofen to cause rashes.   _____

Lesson 33

A

— — — — — — — — — — — — — — — — — — — —

— — — — — — — — — — — — — — — — — — — — — —

— — — — — — — — — — — — — — — — — — .

_____

_____

B

1. _____   4. _____

2. _____   5. _____

3. _____   6. _____

C

Write **s** or **es** in the second column.
Then add the morphographs together.

1. worry + _____ = _____

2. pinch + _____ = _____

3. truck + _____ = _____

4. story + _____ = _____

5. stay + _____ = _____

6. copy + _____ = _____

7. poison + _____ = _____

8. study + _____ = _____

9. boy + _____ = _____

10. cry + _____ = _____

Complete the sentences correctly with these words:

whole   write   hole   features   varies   right   weather   morning

1. Caron's experiment failed, but she had the _____ idea.

2. Tony is going to _____ a short story.

3. Our boat won't float because it has a large _____ in it.

4. I can't eat a _____ cake.

5. Murphy's Cafe _____ fried chicken every Friday.

6. Robin exercises every _____.

7. The _____ in Trinidad rarely _____.

8. Tahiti _____ great _____.

Each sentence has one misspelled word.
Write each word correctly on the blank.

1. The goverment was completely receptive to
   our cause.   _____

2. You'll need to drive strait when you reach the lights.   _____

3. The treatment that Tim was to receive woryed him.   _____

Lesson 34

A

1. _____

_____

2. _____

_____

B

order   style   count   type   tour   beauty

C

Circle each short word that ends in **cvc.**

Remember: The letters **y** and **w** are vowel letters at the end of a morphograph.

The letter **x** acts like two consonant letters.

Short words have 3 or 4 letters.

1. gain	5. fur	9. box	13. drip
2. know	6. show	10. trap	14. tax
3. spin	7. boy	11. brother	15. flop
4. spirit	8. swim	12. win	16. cover

Add the morphographs together. Be careful.
Some of the words follow 2 spelling rules.

1. edge + y + ness   = _____
2. lone + ly + est   = _____
3. re + cept + ion   = _____
4. beauty + ful   = _____
5. fury + ous   = _____
6. shine + y + est   = _____
7. city + es   = _____
8. noise + y + ly   = _____
9. spot + y   = _____
10. fury + ous + ly   = _____

E

Each sentence has one misspelled word.
Write each word correctly on the blank.

1. The boxes were filled with brushs and watches.   _____

2. That glorious day at prescool was the happiest day   _____
   of her life.

3. Kim had been so thirsty that the sight of water made   _____
   her joyus.

Lesson 35 is a test lesson.
There is no worksheet.

Lesson 36

A

1. do not = _____

2. we will = _____

3. were not = _____

4. let us = _____

5. here is = _____

6. are not = _____

7. they will = _____

8. they are = _____

B

Fill in the blanks to show the morphographs in each word.

1. _____ + _____ + _____ = inspection

2. _____ + _____ + _____ = easiest

3. _____ + _____ = beautiful

4. _____ + _____ + _____ = container

5. _____ + _____ + _____ + _____ = exceptional

6. _____ + _____ + _____ = protection

7. _____ + _____ + _____ = relative

8. _____ + _____ + _____ = joyously

9. _____ + _____ + _____ = cloudiness

10. _____ + _____ + _____ = trials

Write **s** or **es** in the second column.
Then add the morphographs together.

1. fly   + _____ = _____

2. search + _____ = _____

3. union + _____ = _____

4. dress + _____ = _____

5. carry + _____ = _____

6. reach + _____ = _____

7. deny   + _____ = _____

8. brush + _____ = _____

9. box   + _____ = _____

10. play   + _____ = _____

Each sentence has one misspelled word.
Write each word correctly on the blank.

1. Did you preview the progect before you rejected it?   _____

2. The first person who passes the goal claimes
   the prize.   _____

3. She was too pasive to make plans about where
   to settle.   _____

Lesson 37

A

1. _____
2. _____
3. _____
4. _____
5. _____

B

Make eight real words from the morphographs in the box.

ly	glory	nerve	ous	joy	study	vary

1. _____
2. _____
3. _____
4. _____
5. _____
6. _____
7. _____
8. _____

C

Write the contractions for the words below.

1. that is   = _____
2. we are   = _____
3. should not = _____
4. they will   = _____
5. they have = _____
6. who is   = _____
7. can not   = _____
8. could not   = _____

D

Add the morphographs together.

1. force + ful + ly   = _____
2. friend + ly + ness   = _____
3. in + tent + ion   = _____
4. re + fuse + al   = _____
5. dis + charge + ed   = _____
6. story + es   = _____
7. please + ure   = _____
8. fury + ous + ly   = _____
9. pro + gress + ive + ly   = _____
10. dis + count + s   = _____

E

Each sentence has one misspelled word.
Write each word correctly on the blank.

1. I have a famous relativ who has many riches.   _____

2. An unexpected, poisonus gas presented a danger.   _____

3. I take my time doing my taxes, exept when I'm
   expecting a refund.   _____

Lesson 38

A

1. _____

   _____

2. _____

   _____

B

1. _____   4. _____

2. _____   5. _____

3. _____   6. _____

C

Write the correct word for each sentence.

1. I poked a **hole/whole** in my worksheet.   _____

2. Would you care for a **peace/piece** of pie?   _____

3. Robin didn't **hear/here** the question.   _____

4. **Too/Two** police officers visited our school.   _____

5. Our house became **vary/very** warm.   _____

6. The dog's **tail/tale** is short.   _____

7. Please **right/write** me a letter.   _____

8. We went **to/too** see a play.   _____

Write **s** or **es** in the second column.
Then add the morphographs together.

1. spray   + _____ = _____

2. catch   + _____ = _____

3. vary   + _____ = _____

4. dry   + _____ = _____

5. stretch + _____ = _____

6. hurry   + _____ = _____

7. stay   + _____ = _____

8. glass   + _____ = _____

Add the morphographs together.

1. dis + please + ing   = _____

2. speed + y + est   = _____

3. re + spect + ful   = _____

4. danger + ous + ly   = _____

5. in + crease + ing + ly = _____

6. please + ure   = _____

Lesson 39

1. _____

_____

2. _____

_____

B

1. _____   4. _____

2. _____   5. _____

3. _____   6. _____

C

Write the correct spelling for each word.
Then write one of these letters after each number.

Write **O** if the word is spelled by just putting the morphographs together.
Write **A** if the final-**e** rule explains why the spelling is changed.
Write **B** if the doubling rule explains why the spelling is changed.
Write **C** if the **y**-to-**i** rule explains why the spelling is changed.

1. _____ place + ment = _____

2. _____ plan + ed   = _____

3. _____ large + ly   = _____

4. _____ deny + al   = _____

5. _____ get + ing   = _____

6. _____ worry + er   = _____

7. _____ spot + less   = _____

8. _____ rage + ing   = _____

9. _____ dog + y   = _____

10. _____ play + er   = _____

Circle the misspelled word in each group.
Then write it correctly on the line.

1. feature
   ditch
   poisonus
   flying
   _____

2. hopeful
   blissful
   stopper
   sieze
   _____

3. portabel
   contain
   dislike
   trapped
   _____

4. ledge
   photograf
   shouldn't
   passage
   _____

5. rental
   worker
   preveiw
   actively
   _____

6. finest
   conserve
   perserve
   reserve
   _____

7. lightly
   catching
   hotest
   driest
   _____

8. hopefulnes
   thoughtful
   restlessness
   throughout
   _____

Each sentence has one misspelled word.
Write each word correctly on the blank.

1. The crys of the babies stopped when they saw the toys.   _____

2. Everyone tries to be respectful of their unyon.   _____

3. The boys are picking beries near the river.   _____

Lesson 40 is a test lesson.
There is no worksheet.

Lesson 41

A

ready   build   bought   simple   cross   chance

B

1. _____   4. _____

2. _____   5. _____

3. _____

C

Write the contractions for the words below.

1. were not = _____   5. are not = _____

2. they will = _____   6. did not = _____

3. does not = _____   7. they are = _____

4. I have   = _____   8. we have = _____

Add the morphographs together.

1. state + ion = _____

2. vise + ion = _____

3. physic + al = _____

4. re + sent + ed = _____

5. spin + er = _____

6. heave + y = _____

7. re + quest + ing = _____

8. duty + es = _____

9. mis + shape + en = _____

10. fame + ous = _____

11. real + ly = _____

12. re + late + ion = _____

E

Draw a line from each word to its clue.

whole •   • I'm going to _____ a report.

hole •   • something great

feat •   • We dug a _____ in the ground.

right •   • also

write •   • all parts together

too •   • My _____ are sore from jogging.

feet •   • Don't turn left. Turn _____.

Lesson 42

chief   niece   brief   grief   thief

1. _____   4. _____

2. _____   5. _____

3. _____

Fill in the blanks to show the morphographs in each word.

1. _____ + _____ = expel

2. _____ + _____ + _____ = refusal

3. _____ + _____ = pleasure

4. _____ + _____ = chiefly

5. _____ + _____ + _____ = respectable

6. _____ + _____ + _____ + _____ = misconception

7. _____ + _____ + _____ = descriptive

8. _____ + _____ = statement

9. _____ + _____ = station

10. _____ + _____ + _____ = relative

11. _____ + _____ + _____ = reinstate

12. _____ + _____ + _____ = ripening

Make nine real words from the morphographs in the box.

ed	cover	un	re	dis	solve

1. _____   6. _____

2. _____   7. _____

3. _____   8. _____

4. _____   9. _____

5. _____

Lesson 43

A

The committee had high regard for honesty and courage.

_____

_____

B

1. _____   5. _____

2. _____   6. _____

3. _____   7. _____

4. _____   8. _____

C

Write **s** or **es** in the second column.
Then add the morphographs together.

1. stay + _____ = _____

2. story + _____ = _____

3. try   + _____ = _____

4. reach + _____ = _____

5. cross + _____ = _____

6. city + _____ = _____

7. ditch + _____ = _____

8. deny + _____ = _____

These words are in the puzzle.
Circle seven or more of the words.

k	t	n	k	n	o	w
f	r	i	d	c	w	r
d	a	e	n	h	i	a
k	i	c	j	i	n	p
n	d	e	t	e	c	t
f	l	y	t	f	c	y
h	e	r	o	i	c	t

fact	know	wrap
diet	chief	heroic
win	fly	detect
tin	niece	reject

E

Fill in the blanks to show the morphographs in each word.

1. _____ + _____ + _____ = produced

2. _____ + _____ = repel

3. _____ + _____ = devise

4. _____ + _____ + _____ = revision

5. _____ + _____ + _____ = artistic

6. _____ + _____ + _____ = disrespect

7. _____ + _____ + _____ = protection

F

Each sentence has one misspelled word.
Write each word correctly on the blank.

1. The work on the new bridge is ready for its fisical   _____
   inspection.

2. Major cities are planning better highway   _____
   developement.

3. Her refusal to read the sience book was   _____
   questionable.

Lesson 44

A

___ ___ __ m m __ t t __ __ ___ ___ ___

___ a __ __ ___ ___ h __ e __ y ___

___ ___ __ o u ___ ___ ___ .

_____

_____

B

1. _____   4. _____

2. _____   5. _____

3. _____   6. _____

C

Cross out the misspelled words in these sentences.
Then write the words correctly above the crossed-out words.

My sience teacher is vary intresting.

A reporter photografed the frigthened people.

His mother bougth a simpley beautyful dress.

There reasoning was'nt logical.

The reporter hired a detective for protecion.

Goverment should protect the rites of people.

Add the morphographs together.

1. create + ion   = _____

2. style + ish + ly   = _____

3. dis + solve + ing   = _____

4. un + re + vise + ed   = _____

5. type + ic + al   = _____

6. re + cept + ion   = _____

7. de + part + ure   = _____

8. de + cept + ive   = _____

9. mis + place + ed   = _____

10. re + strict + ion   = _____

11. beauty + ful + ly   = _____

12. photo + graph + y   = _____

Each sentence has one misspelled word.
Write each word correctly on the blank.

1. Who's that player who catchs so well?   _____

2. Long trials make the judge nervus.   _____

3. Our intention was to dissarm the intruder.   _____

Lesson 45 is a test lesson.
There is no worksheet.

Lesson 46

A

_ _ _ _ _ _ _ m _ _ t _ _ _ _ _ _ _ _ _ _ _ _ _

_ _ _ _ _ _ _ _ _ _ _ _ _ e _ _ _ _

_ _ _ _ _ u _ _ _ _ _ .

_____

_____

B

1. _____   5. _____

2. _____   6. _____

3. _____   7. _____

4. _____   8. _____

C

Complete the sentences correctly with these words.

right   too   to   tale   various   their   there   tail

1. Martin's desk is often covered with _____ things.

2. Ellen always knows the _____ thing to say.

3. We used rags to make a _____ for her kite.

4. Ana had the _____ answers for all the questions.

5. Helen and Charles built _____ own bicycle.

6. Terry's _____ about pirates was _____ far-fetched for me.

7. I would like you _____ put the books over _____.

D

Write the correct spelling for each word.
Then write one of these letters after each number.

Write **O** if the word is spelled by just putting the morphographs together.
Write **A** if the final-**e** rule explains why the spelling is changed.
Write **B** if the doubling rule explains why the spelling is changed.
Write **C** if the **y**-to-**i** rule explains why the spelling is changed.

1. _____ ready + ness = _____

2. _____ sad + ness = _____

3. _____ large + ly = _____

4. _____ style + ish = _____

5. _____ edge + ing = _____

6. _____ class + ic + al = _____

7. _____ type + ic + al = _____

8. _____ hope + ing = _____

9. _____ hop + ing = _____

10. _____ duty + es = _____

11. _____ force + ful = _____

12. _____ boy + ish = _____

E

Each sentence has one misspelled word.
Write each word correctly on the blank.

1. You shouldn't wash your silk dreses.   _____

2. Let's look over that ledje.   _____

3. Today's displeasing temperature and clowdiness   _____
   made everyone unhappy.

Lesson 47

A

1. _____

   _____

2. _____

   _____

B

1. _____ 4. _____

2. _____ 5. _____

3. _____

C

_____

_____

_____

_____

_____

_____

_____

_____

_____

Fill in the blanks to show the morphographs in each word.

1. _____ + _____ + _____ = producing

2. _____ + _____ + _____ = stylishly

3. _____ + _____ = simplest

4. _____ + _____ + _____ = protective

5. _____ + _____ + _____ = relation

6. _____ + _____ + _____ = designer

7. _____ + _____ = resign

8. _____ + _____ = signal

Lesson 48

A

today   yesterday   tomorrow   afternoon   evening

B

Some explorers discovered treasure on a magic island.

_____

_____

C

1. _____   4. _____

2. _____   5. _____

3. _____

D

Add the morphographs together.

1. create + ive   = _____

2. create + ion   = _____

3. re + create + ion   = _____

4. dis + courage   = _____

5. re + gard + less   = _____

6. niece + es   = _____

7. re + quest +ed   = _____

8. in + tense + ive + ly = _____

These words are in the puzzle.
Circle seven or more of the words.

doubt	loan	plot
quote	bone	madly
state	louder	nasty
moss	agree	went

d	p	m	q	u	e
m	o	l	o	a	n
a	q	o	o	s	a
d	o	u	b	t	s
l	o	d	o	a	t
y	w	e	n	t	y
a	g	r	e	e	e

Each sentence has one misspelled word.
Write each word correctly on the blank.

1. Mom agreed that we'er getting new glasses today. _____

2. The tourists from various countries traveled joyusly _____
   together.

3. We can catch bugs and put them in this contaner. _____

Lesson 49

A

_ o _ _ _ _ _ o r e _ _ _ _ s c o _ _ _ _ _ _

_ _ e a s _ _ _ _ _ _ _ _ _ g _ _ _ s _ _ _ _ .

_____

_____

B

1. _____

2. _____

3. _____

4. _____

5. _____

6. _____

C

_____

_____

_____

_____

_____

_____

_____

_____

_____

Write the contractions for the words below.

1. they had = _____
2. we are = _____
3. it is = _____
4. do not = _____
5. what is = _____

6. you will = _____
7. are not = _____
8. they are = _____
9. we have = _____
10. she will = _____

Circle the misspelled word in each group.
Then write it correctly on the line.

1. breakable
   dowbt
   pleasure
   peaceful

2. increase
   changing
   noisily
   taxs

3. exchange
   chance
   wreckage
   sturdyness

4. honesty
   tomorow
   inspect
   product

_____ _____ _____ _____

Each sentence has one misspelled word.
Write each word correctly on the blank.

1. I bought a very basik yet artistic house.   _____

2. Sue had a brief chance to meet the comittee.   _____

3. The chief gave us a grafic description of the incident.   _____

Lesson 50 is a test lesson.
There is no worksheet.

Lesson 51

A

_ _ _ _ _ _ _ _ _ _ e _ _ _ _ _ _ _ _ _ _ _

_ _ a s _ _ _ _ _ _ _ _ _ g _ _ _ s _ _ _ .

_____

_____

B

1. _____   4. _____

2. _____   5. _____

3. _____   6. _____

C

Add the morphographs together.

1. trans + gress + ion   = _____

2. pre + fer   = _____

3. dis + courage + ment = _____

4. fine + ish + ed   = _____

5. soft + en + ing   = _____

6. con + quest + s   = _____

7. in + flame + ed   = _____

8. scare + y + est   = _____

9. tribe + al   = _____

10. clean + ly + ness   = _____

11. stress + ful   = _____

12. de + sign + er   = _____

D

Draw a line from each word to its clue.

sale •

weather •

their •

there •

they're •

whether •

piece •

pain •

• The Smiths keep _____ dog outside.

• they are

• a part of something

• cold and cloudy

• I'm going _____ Dawn does or not.

• lower prices

• Tim has a _____ in his knee.

• The pencil sharpener is over _____.

E

Each sentence has one misspelled word.
Write each word correctly on the blank.

1. The oil Ted discovered is thicker than tipical oil.   _____

2. My neice is building a simple home.   _____

3. He will look foolish if he dosen't revise this text.   _____

Lesson 52

A

1. _____

_____

2. _____

_____

B

1. _____   4. _____

2. _____   5. _____

3. _____

C

Fill in the circle marked **R** if the underlined word is spelled right.
Fill in the circle marked **W** if the underlined word is spelled wrong.

1. Their actions showed great <u>coorage</u>.   Ⓡ   Ⓦ

2. The <u>comittee</u> has made its decision.   Ⓡ   Ⓦ

3. Pauline is the <u>luckiest</u> person I know.   Ⓡ   Ⓦ

4. <u>Governments</u> are made up of people.   Ⓡ   Ⓦ

5. It is <u>to</u> warm outside to snow.   Ⓡ   Ⓦ

6. Running is good <u>exercise</u>.   Ⓡ   Ⓦ

Fill in the blanks to show the morphographs in each word.

1. _____ + _____ + _____ = realistic

2. _____ + _____ + _____ = translation

3. _____ + _____ + _____ = disgraceful

4. _____ + _____ + _____ = spherical

5. _____ + _____ + _____ = production

6. _____ + _____ + _____ = disrespect

7. _____ + _____ + _____ = prescription

8. _____ + _____ = texture

9. _____ + _____ + _____ = trickiest

10. _____ + _____ + _____ = furiously

Circle each short word that ends in **cvc.**

Remember: The letters **y** and **w** are vowel letters at the end
of a morphograph.

The letter **x** acts like two consonant letters.

Short words have 3 or 4 letters.

1. drop	**4.** fix	**7.** jar	**10.** danger
2. flaw	**5.** trip	**8.** pool	**11.** stray
3. plan	**6.** major	**9.** shop	**12.** spin

Lesson 53

A

Fill in the circle marked **R** if the underlined word is spelled right.
Fill in the circle marked **W** if the underlined word is spelled wrong.

1. Anne's father goes to school in the <u>evning</u>. (R) (W)
2. Someone forgot to <u>clothes</u> the door. (R) (W)
3. Lisa's <u>honisty</u> always paid off. (R) (W)
4. I don't understand Bob's <u>edginess</u>. (R) (W)
5. We formed a <u>commitee</u> to plan the party. (R) (W)
6. Have you finished <u>writing</u> your report? (R) (W)

B

1. _____ 5. _____
2. _____ 6. _____
3. _____ 7. _____
4. _____ 8. _____

C

Make twelve real words from the morphographs in the box.

fer	scribe	trans	pre	port	con	de	re	serve

1. _____ 7. _____
2. _____ 8. _____
3. _____ 9. _____
4. _____ 10. _____
5. _____ 11. _____
6. _____ 12. _____

Figure out the rules and write them.

cvc and the next . . . in a short word when the . . . double the final **c** . . . word ends . . . morphograph begins with **v**

_____

_____

and the next morphograph . . . to **i** in a word when the . . . change the **y** . . . word ends consonant-and-**y** . . . begins with anything except **i**

_____

_____

Fill in the blanks to show the morphographs in each word.

1. _____ + _____ + _____ = exception

2. _____ + _____ = expel

3. _____ + _____ + _____ = provision

4. _____ + _____ + _____ = transaction

5. _____ + _____ = dispel

6. _____ + _____ + _____ = container

Lesson 54

A

tragic   comic   critic   medic   pulse

B

1. _____

_____

2. _____

_____

C

1. _____ 4. _____

2. _____ 5. _____

3. _____ 6. _____

D

Add the morphographs together.

1. dis + pose + al   = _____

2. pro + duct + ion   = _____

3. pro + vise + ion   = _____

4. ready + ly   = _____

5. critic + al   = _____

6. type + ic +al   = _____

7. ex + cept + ion + al   = _____

8. fine + al + ly   = _____

9. athlete + ic   = _____

10. mis + in + form + ed   = _____

11. peace + ful + ly   = _____

12. photo + graph + y   = _____

Write **s** or **es** in the second column.
Then add the morphographs together.

1. loss   + _____ = _____

2. tray   + _____ = _____

3. puppy   + _____ = _____

4. bench   + _____ = _____

5. evening + _____ = _____

6. wish   + _____ = _____

7. monkey + _____ = _____

8. body   + _____ = _____

Each sentence has one misspelled word.
Write each word correctly on the blank.

1. Tom resented the simple revison that Bill made.   _____

2. Unresolved greif doesn't go away.   _____

3. I beleive I've misplaced two packages.   _____

> Lesson 55 is a test lesson.
> There is no worksheet.

Lesson 56

A

show   blow   know   grow   throw   draw

B

1. _____   4. _____

2. _____   5. _____

3. _____

C

_____

_____

_____

_____

_____

_____

_____

_____

D

Write the correct word for each sentence.

1. Martin always hangs up his **close/clothes.** _____

2. I don't **know/no** the answer. _____

3. Our club **meats/meets** after school. _____

4. There is a **loan/lone** tree growing in our yard. _____

5. The tickets will be for **sail/sale** in the morning. _____

6. We can't **hear/here** the music. _____

Add the morphographs together.

1. comic + al   = _____

2. ex + pose + ure   = _____

3. dis + courage + ment = _____

4. sculpt + ure   = _____

5. trans + late + ed   = _____

6. ex + press + ive   = _____

7. pro + pose + al   = _____

8. de + fine + ing   = _____

Each sentence has one misspelled word.
Write each word correctly on the blank.

1. We searched trughout the state to discover a new star._____

2. Her vision of the future dosen't seem foolish to me.   _____

3. I was distracted and missplaced my contract.   _____

Lesson 57

A

1. _____   5. _____

2. _____   6. _____

3. _____   7. _____

4. _____   8. _____

B

Fill in the blanks to show the morphographs in each word.

1. _____ + _____ + _____ = invention

2. _____ + _____ + _____ = disposal

3. _____ + _____ + _____ = appraisal

4. _____ + _____ + _____ = transaction

5. _____ + _____ + _____ + _____ = undiscovered

6. _____ + _____ = chancy

7. _____ + _____ + _____ = dangerously

8. _____ + _____ + _____ + _____ = increasingly

C

These words are in the puzzle.
Circle seven or more of the words.

blow   fill   athlete

team   often   city

loan   flaw   head

taxes   noun   produce

a	t	o	f	t	e	n
t	t	b	i	e	f	o
c	a	h	l	a	l	u
i	x	e	l	o	a	n
t	e	a	m	e	w	o
y	s	d	o	e	t	e
p	r	o	d	u	c	e

Lesson 58

A

rhythm   cycle   sphere

B

1. _____

_____

2. _____

_____

C

_____

_____

_____

_____

_____

_____

_____

_____

_____

D

cause   island   provision   prevention

explore   questionable   describe   through

doubtful   frightening   exposure   increases

E

Fill in the circle marked **R** if the underlined word is spelled right.
Fill in the circle marked **W** if the underlined word is spelled wrong.

1. Lee would like to be a television <u>critic</u>.   (R) (W)
2. We can <u>apoint</u> three people to the committee. (R) (W)
3. Who remembered to <u>cloze</u> the door?   (R) (W)
4. I enjoy history and <u>sciense</u>.   (R) (W)
5. My parents <u>approve</u> of my hobbies.   (R) (W)
6. Cora's mother went to a <u>convention</u> in Paris.   (R) (W)
7. We can <u>dispoze</u> of old business quickly.   (R) (W)
8. The Massons love <u>there</u> new house.   (R) (W)

F

Each sentence has one misspelled word.
Write each word correctly on the blank.

1. Requesting a text revision is tipical at this stage.   _____

2. If we don't meet her demands, she'll resine.   _____

3. We have the job of transporting an invaluble treasure. _____

There are no worksheets for
Lesson 59 and Lesson 60.

Lesson 61

merge   ground   sleep   shame   while

B

Two scientists and their assistants were in the automobile accident.

_____

_____

C

1. sew + en = _____
2. know + en = _____
3. ripe + en = _____
4. show + en = _____

5. prove + en = _____
6. grow + en = _____
7. throw + en = _____
8. gold + en = _____

D

Add the morphographs together.

1. con + tent + s   = _____
2. in + vent + ion   = _____
3. re + verse + al   = _____
4. ap + point + ment   = _____
5. trans + fer   = _____
6. rhythm + ic   = _____
7. pro + pose + al   = _____
8. in + tent + ion   = _____
9. ex + pel   = _____
10. sleep + less + ness = _____
11. rain + y + est   = _____
12. hot + est   = _____

E

Draw a line from each word to its clue.

sew •

clothes •

right •

close •

write •

piece •

sow •

peace •

• Jean's new _____ look nice.

• You should _____ to your grandmother.

• needle and thread

• All the countries signed a _____ treaty.

• Please _____ the window.

• put seeds in the ground

• not wrong

• part of something

F

Each sentence has one misspelled word.
Write each word correctly on the blank.

1. The monkys became nervous and distracted by the _____
   end of the show.

2. His leg was inflamed after the tradgic accident. _____

3. She has a respectable job in the field of photoraphy. _____

Lesson 62

A

___ _cie___st_ ___ __ei_
_s__sta___ _e__ __ __
_u_____ile _cc__e__.

_____

_____

B

1. _____   5. _____

2. _____   6. _____

3. _____   7. _____

4. _____   8. _____

C

Add the morphographs together.
Remember to use the rule about adding **en.**

1. draw + en = _____   5. strength + en = _____

2. loose + en = _____   6. threat + en = _____

3. blow + en = _____   7. sew + en = _____

4. know + en = _____   8. grow + en = _____

D

Make eighteen real words from the morphographs in the box.

ing	serve	tain	con	re	fine	form	de

1. _____
2. _____
3. _____
4. _____
5. _____
6. _____
7. _____
8. _____
9. _____
10. _____
11. _____
12. _____
13. _____
14. _____
15. _____
16. _____
17. _____
18. _____

F

Each sentence has one misspelled word.
Write each word correctly on the blank.

1. She looked more boyish in athletic cloths.   _____

2. She refussed to take a prescription drug for her
   treatment.   _____

3. The last athlete finaly finished the race.   _____

Lesson 63

_ _

_ _ _ _ _ _ _ _ _ _ _ _ _ _ _ _ _ _ _ _

_ _ _ _ _ _ _ _ _ _ _ _ _ _ _ _ _ _ .

_____

_____

B

1. _____   5. _____

2. _____   6. _____

3. _____   7. _____

4. _____   8. _____

C

Fill in the blanks to show the morphographs in each word.

1. _____ + _____ + _____ = shamefully

2. _____ + _____ + _____ = extension

3. _____ + _____ + _____ = provision

4. _____ + _____ + _____ = prevention

5. _____ + _____ + _____ + _____ = intentional

6. _____ + _____ + _____ = disposable

7. _____ + _____ + _____ = disclosure

8. _____ + _____ = denial

9. _____ + _____ + _____ = rejection

10. _____ + _____ + _____ = description

D

Circle the misspelled word in each group.
Then write it correctly on the line.

1. reqwest

   revision

   while

   feature

   _____

2. basic

   quoteable

   dangerous

   reverse

   _____

3. breifly

   physical

   spinning

   tomorrow

   _____

4. transfer

   photograph

   straight

   heavyest

   _____

5. science

   committee

   intrested

   duties

   _____

6. worried

   showen

   cloudiness

   pleasure

   _____

Lesson 64

1. _____

_____

2. _____

_____

B

1. fer	**5.** skid	**9.** win	**13.** grab
2. vent	**6.** tragic	**10.** draw	**14.** cover
3. flat	**7.** pel	**11.** spirit	**15.** spray
4. blow	**8.** cap	**12.** ject	**16.** cut

C

Add the morphographs together.
Remember to use your spelling rules.

1. rhythm + ic + al   = _____

2. draw + en   = _____

3. for + give + en   = _____

4. un + in + tend + ed = _____

5. in + tent + ion + al   = _____

6. grow + en   = _____

7. shop + er   = _____

8. vent + ure + ed   = _____

9. ease + y + ly   = _____

10. ex + pose + ure   = _____

D

These words are in the puzzle.
Circle seven or more of
the words.

shake   scope   thousand

athlete   niece   equal

under   friend   voice

transact   seed   farm

a	t	h	s	v	o	i	c	e
a	t	h	l	e	t	e	a	v
f	s	c	o	p	e	v	s	e
r	a	h	v	u	n	d	e	r
i	t	r	a	n	s	a	c	t
e	v	s	m	k	f	a	e	a
n	i	e	c	e	e	s	n	a
d	n	e	e	q	u	a	l	d

E

Each sentence has one misspelled word.
Write each word correctly on the blank.

1. In photography, light exposeure is important,
   regardless of the time of day.   _____

2. Let me show you how to make a beutiful
   glass sphere.   _____

3. Mom is hurrying to finish sewing her formil gown. _____

Lesson 65 is a test lesson.
There is no worksheet.

Lesson 66

A

1. _____

2. _____

B

1. _____ 4. _____

2. _____ 5. _____

3. _____ 6. _____

C

D

Write **s** or **es** in the second column.
Then add the morphographs together.

1. trophy + _____ = _____
2. fox + _____ = _____
3. lily + _____ = _____
4. ground + _____ = _____
5. peach + _____ = _____
6. pony + _____ = _____
7. crash + _____ = _____
8. monkey + _____ = _____

E

Fill in the blanks to show the morphographs in each word.

1. _____ + _____ + _____ + _____ = misinformed
2. _____ + _____ + _____ = carelessly
3. _____ + _____ + _____ = cheerfulness
4. _____ + _____ + _____ = instruction
5. _____ + _____ + _____ = reaction
6. _____ + _____ + _____ = descriptive
7. _____ + _____ + _____ = pretending
8. _____ + _____ + _____ = appointment
9. _____ + _____ + _____ = unbreakable
10. _____ + _____ + _____ = spherical
11. _____ + _____ = worthy
12. _____ + _____ + _____ = tightening

Lesson 67

A

1. _____

   _____

2. _____

   _____

B

1. _____   5. _____

2. _____   6. _____

3. _____   7. _____

4. _____   8. _____

C

Choose two words from the list to complete each sentence.

write	seen	scene	close	threw
vary	clothes	through	very	right

1. Bonnie and Wayne found the _____ _____ for winter.

2. I have _____ many stars _____ my telescope.

3. I like to _____ the _____ that I'm painting.

4. The salesman _____ in a free trip to _____ the sale.

5. Jane has _____ Chan _____ his name in Chinese.

D

Add the morphographs together.

1. fail + ure = _____

2. trans + plant = _____

3. wake + en + ing = _____

4. con + struct + ion = _____

5. build + ing = _____

6. in + tent + ion = _____

7. re + tain + ed = _____

8. de + cept + ion = _____

9. sub + merge = _____

10. ex + cept + ion + al = _____

11. pro + tect + ive = _____

12. art + ist + ic = _____

13. trans + late + ed = _____

14. de + part + ure = _____

E

Each sentence has one misspelled word.
Write each word correctly on the blank.

1. How do you propose to design this mision? _____

2. The typist doesn't aprove of the content of the paper. _____

3. The commissioner was very criticle of the designer. _____

Lesson 68

A

pound　　　habit　　　saint　　　brother　　　sister　　　false

B

1. _____   4. _____

2. _____   5. _____

3. _____   6. _____

C

_____

_____

_____

_____

_____

_____

_____

_____

D

Write the correct spelling for each word.
Then write one of these letters after each number.

Write **O** if the word is spelled by just putting the morphographs together.
Write **A** if the final-**e** rule explains why the spelling is changed.
Write **B** if the doubling rule explains why the spelling is changed.
Write **C** if the **y**-to-**i** rule explains why the spelling is changed.

1. _____ vary + ous = _____
2. _____ cycle + ist = _____
3. _____ get + ing = _____
4. _____ pay + ment = _____
5. _____ state + ment = _____
6. _____ type + ist = _____
7. _____ live + ly + ness = _____
8. _____ fury + ous = _____
9. _____ skin + ed = _____
10. _____ friend + ly + est = _____
11. _____ cube + ic = _____
12. _____ beauty + ful = _____

E

Cross out the misspelled words in these sentences.
Then write the words correctly above the crossed-out words.

I wood like to toor a seenic iland.

He took a chanse when he crossed that old brige.

Lesson 69

A

1. _____
_____

2. _____
_____

B

1. _____   4. _____

2. _____   5. _____

3. _____   6. _____

C

Make nine real words from the morphographs in the box.

tract	con	ject	in	ion	duct	re

1. _____   6. _____

2. _____   7. _____

3. _____   8. _____

4. _____   9. _____

5. _____

Fill in the blanks to show the morphographs in each word.

1. _____ + _____ = falsely

2. _____ + _____ + _____ = insisted

3. _____ + _____ + _____ = subtraction

4. _____ + _____ + _____ + _____ = respectfully

5. _____ + _____ + _____ = reversal

6. _____ + _____ + _____ = recreation

7. _____ + _____ + _____ = resigned

8. _____ + _____ + _____ = objective

Cross out the misspelled words in these sentences.
Then write the words correctly above the crossed-out words.

An unknowen athelete defeated the famus runner.

I have progresed wonderfully with my science project.

Lesson 70 is a test lesson.
There is no worksheet.

Lesson 71

1. logic + ly = _____

2. proud + ly = _____

3. graph + ic + ly = _____

4. real + ly = _____

5. nice + ly = _____

6. athlete + ic + ly = _____

B

1. _____   **4.** _____

2. _____   **5.** _____

3. _____

C

cyclist	assistant	rhythm	accident
productive	proposal	extension	habit
around	structure	automobile	falsely

D

Add the morphographs together.

1. per + sist + ed   = _____

2. dis + tract + ion   = _____

3. a + wake + en   = _____

4. pro + tect + ion   = _____

5. ob + serve + ing   = _____

6. ex + press + ion   = _____

7. con + tent + ment   = _____

8. un + ap + prove + ed   = _____

9. storm + y + ness   = _____

10. de + light + ful   = _____

E

Draw a line from each word to its clue.

sow •   • I forgot to _____ the closet door.

scene •   • what you wear

close •   • The sun on the water made a beautiful _____ .

tail •   • also

clothes •   • Did you put those things _____ ?

their •   • plant seeds

there •   • I think _____ coming home soon.

they're •   • The dogs are scratching _____ fleas.

too •   • Our cat doesn't have a _____ .

There is no worksheet
for Lesson 72.

Lesson 73

A

That student appears to be thorough and conscientious.

_____

_____

B

Add the morphographs together.
Remember the rule about adding **al** before **ly.**

1. critic + ly   = _____
2. cost + ly   = _____
3. hero + ic + ly   = _____
4. magic + ly   = _____
5. firm + ly   = _____
6. rhythm + ic + ly = _____
7. chief + ly   = _____
8. comic + ly   = _____

C

1. _____   4. _____

2. _____   5. _____

3. _____   6. _____

D

Add the morphographs together.

1. per + fect + ion = _____

2. com + press + ion = _____

3. ob + serve + er = _____

4. a + ground = _____

5. re + sist + ed = _____

6. sub + merge + ed = _____

7. in + struct + ion + al = _____

8. per + form + er = _____

9. ob + long = _____

10. a + long = _____

11. ob + ject + ion = _____

12. sub + tract + ion = _____

E

Each sentence has one misspelled word.
Write each word correctly on the blank.

1. Please forgive me for forgetting my apointment. _____

2. The waves extended out in a rythmical pattern. _____

3. The automobile was defective and could cause an acident. _____

4. Can you easiley define the contents of the contract? _____

Lesson 74

_ _ _ _   _ _ _ _   e _ _   _ _ p e a _ _   _ _   _ _

_ _ o r o u _ _   _ _ _   _ _ _ s c i _ _ t i _ _ _ .

_____

_____

B

1. _____   4. _____

2. _____   5. _____

3. _____

C

1. _____

_____

2. _____

_____

D

Add the morphographs together.
Remember to use the rule about adding **al** before **ly**.

1. strict + ly   = _____

2. graph + ic + ly   = _____

3. physic + ly   = _____

4. round + ly   = _____

5. critic + ly   = _____

6. athlete + ic + ly = _____

7. like + ly   = _____

8. danger + ous + ly = _____

E

Circle the misspelled word in each group.
Then write it correctly on the line.

1. useless

   realy

   changing

   strength

   _____

2. sleepyness

   athletic

   furious

   basic

   _____

3. nineteen

   fashion

   version

   cheif

   _____

4. photograph

   vizion

   breathless

   spirit

   _____

5. sieze

   duties

   request

   settle

   _____

6. straight

   explain

   hopefully

   thrown

   _____

Lesson 75 is a test lesson.
There is no worksheet.

Lesson 76

_ _

_ .

_____

_____

B

loaf   calf   half   shelf   wolf

C

_____

_____

_____

_____

_____

_____

_____

_____

_____

_____

D

Fill in the blanks to show the morphographs in each word.

1. _____ + _____ = spiritual

2. _____ + _____ = recur

3. _____ + _____ = compile

4. _____ + _____ + _____ = perfection

5. _____ + _____ + _____ = awaken

6. _____ + _____ + _____ = performer

7. _____ + _____ = insist

8. _____ + _____ + _____ = contraction

9. _____ + _____ + _____ + _____ = objectionable

10. _____ + _____ + _____ = destructive

11. _____ + _____ + _____ = forgiven

12. _____ + _____ + _____ = exposure

E

Each sentence has one misspelled word.
Write each word correctly on the blank.

1. What a shame that the hottest days were also the dryest days! _____

2. The ponies were graceful and quik. _____

3. Any failur to perform will end your contract. _____

A

wife	life	self	knife	leaf

B

1. _____

_____

2. _____

_____

C

Add the morphographs together.

1. child + hood = _____

2. habit + ual = _____

3. trans + miss + ion = _____

4. de + frost + ing = _____

5. re + create + ion = _____

6. com + miss + ion + er = _____

7. globe + al + ly = _____

8. de + script + ion = _____

9. false + hood = _____

10. a + piece = _____

11. sub + miss + ive = _____

12. per + fect + ion = _____

D

Write the correct word for each sentence.

1. Have you **scene/seen** Mercury or Venus?   _____

2. The sun is shining **threw/through** the window.   _____

3. Our friends will be **hear/here** soon.   _____

4. The students finished **their/they're** work.   _____

5. Turn **right/write** at the corner.   _____

6. I soaked my **feat/feet** after the race.   _____

7. She will **sail/sale** her boat on the river.   _____

8. Do you know how to **sew/sow** buttons?   _____

Lesson 78

A

1. thief _____

2. wife _____

3. loaf _____

4. wolf _____

B

1. _____

_____

2. _____

_____

C

1. _____   5. _____

2. _____   6. _____

3. _____   7. _____

4. _____   8. _____

D

These words are in the puzzle. Circle nine or more of the words.

government	alike	wonder
thousand	shine	cement
sort	graphic	ground
danger	heroic	voters
spend	tend	

g	t	t	w	c	s	h	i	n	e
g	h	t	g	o	e	p	g	t	c
g	o	v	e	r	n	m	e	n	t
r	u	c	o	n	a	d	e	n	e
o	s	o	r	t	d	p	e	n	d
u	a	l	i	k	e	r	h	r	t
n	n	c	c	h	e	r	o	i	c
d	d	a	n	g	e	r	s	m	c

E

Write the contractions for the words below.

1. can not = _____
2. does not = _____
3. you are = _____
4. they will = _____
5. they have = _____
6. could not = _____
7. she is = _____
8. are not = _____

F

Each sentence has one misspelled word.
Write each word correctly on the blank.

1. The instruction was confuseing because it wasn't _____
   worded logically.

2. Foxes have a habbit of smelling the ground near _____
   their homes.

3. What is the objetive of the instruction you are _____
   using?

Lesson 79

A

1. _____

_____

2. _____

_____

B

1. _____ 5. _____

2. _____ 6. _____

3. _____ 7. _____

4. _____ 8. _____

C

Fill in the circle marked **R** if the underlined word is spelled right.
Fill in the circle marked **W** if the underlined word is spelled wrong.

1. Can you <u>discribe</u> a rose? Ⓡ Ⓦ

2. We <u>finished</u> our work early. Ⓡ Ⓦ

3. Some rules have <u>exseptions</u>. Ⓡ Ⓦ

4. I like the <u>mournings</u> more than the afternoons. Ⓡ Ⓦ

5. <u>Ninteen</u> players made the team. Ⓡ Ⓦ

6. He bought a dog for <u>protection</u>. Ⓡ Ⓦ

7. We went to the park <u>instead</u> of the beach. Ⓡ Ⓦ

8. My father often works <u>threwout</u> the night. Ⓡ Ⓦ

Fill in the blanks to show the morphographs in each word.

1. _____ + _____ + _____ = likelihood

2. _____ + _____ + _____ = usually

3. _____ + _____ + _____ = commission

4. _____ + _____ = recur

5. _____ + _____ = transmit

6. _____ + _____ = across

7. _____ + _____ + _____ = submerged

8. _____ + _____ = alone

9. _____ + _____ + _____ = observer

10. _____ + _____ + _____ = disgraceful

11. _____ + _____ + _____ = imperfect

12. _____ + _____ = station

E

Each sentence has one misspelled word.
Write each word correctly on the blank.

1. You're likley to incur a costly fine. _____

2. The performer created a deliteful show. _____

3. The shopper nervousley asked the assistants for help. _____

Lesson 80 is a test lesson.
There is no worksheet.

Lesson 81

A

1. loaf _____
2. shelf _____
3. thief _____
4. wife _____
5. knife _____
6. life _____

B

void   friend   mobile   temple   proper   please

C

1. _____   4. _____
2. _____   5. _____
3. _____

D

Make nine real words from the morphographs in the box.

ob   ed   ject   pro   ion   in   de

1. _____   6. _____
2. _____   7. _____
3. _____   8. _____
4. _____   9. _____
5. _____

E

Add the morphographs together.
Remember to use the rule about adding **al** before **ly**
when the word ends with the letters **ic.**

1. short + ly   = _____

2. hero + ic + ly   = _____

3. class + ic + ly   = _____

4. beauty + ful + ly = _____

5. ethic + ly   = _____

6. strict + ly   = _____

7. logic + ly   = _____

8. rhythm + ic + ly   = _____

Lesson 82

1. _____

   _____

2. _____

   _____

B

C

Circle the short **cvc** morphographs.

1. grab   4. cur   7. mud   10. pel   13. run

2. mit   5. vent   8. fer   11. ship   14. blow

3. tray   6. habit   9. speak   12. magic   15. critic

Add the morphographs together.

1. act + ive + ate = _____

2. ex + tract + ion = _____

3. a + void + able = _____

4. sign + ate + ure = _____

5. ob + struct + ion = _____

6. pro + tect + ion = _____

7. please + ure = _____

8. con + serve + ate + ion = _____

9. re + fuse + al = _____

10. ex + plore + er = _____

11. im + mobile = _____

12. in + form + ate + ive = _____

Lesson 83

Write the plural for each word.
Remember to say the plural word to yourself.

1. leaf _____

2. self _____

3. calf _____

4. knife _____

5. thief _____

6. elf _____

B

pure   temper   vast   tempt   image

C

1. _____   5. _____

2. _____   6. _____

3. _____   7. _____

4. _____   8. _____

D

honesty	drawn	conservation	critical
science	discourage	assistant	basically
treasure	awhile	usually	accident
thoroughly	bought	avoidable	throughout

E

Write the correct spelling for each word.
Then write one of these letters after each number.

Write **O** if the word is spelled by just putting the morphographs together.
Write **A** if the final-**e** rule explains why the spelling is changed.
Write **B** if the doubling rule explains why the spelling is changed.
Write **C** if the **y**-to-**i** rule explains why the spelling is changed.

1. _____ pure + ist = _____

2. _____ clean + ly + ness = _____

3. _____ skid + ed = _____

4. _____ vise + ual = _____

5. _____ salt + y + est = _____

6. _____ shine + ing = _____

7. _____ hurry + ing = _____

8. _____ speed + y + ly = _____

9. _____ grip + s = _____

10. _____ baby + es = _____

F

Each sentence has one misspelled word.
Write each word correctly on the blank.

1. The student's notebook was tradgically submerged in the lake. _____

2. A cold compres basically can help an infection. _____

3. This oblong shape makes a perfect struture. _____

There are no worksheets for
Lesson 84 and Lesson 85.

Lesson 86

A

Their approach to acquiring knowledge fascinates me.

_____

_____

B

1. _____   5. _____

2. _____   6. _____

3. _____   7. _____

4. _____   8. _____

C

Add the morphographs together.

1. de + vast + ate + ing   = _____

2. medic + ate + ion   = _____

3. friend + ly + est   = _____

4. con + fuse + ion   = _____

5. re + ply + ed   = _____

6. pre + script + ion   = _____

7. re + ap + pear   = _____

8. case + ual   = _____

9. comp + press + ion   = _____

10. sub + miss + ion   = _____

11. ob + serve + ate + ion = _____

12. in + form + ate + ive = _____

D

Circle the misspelled word in each group.
Then write it correctly on the line.

1. winner
   veried
   searches
   rhythmically
   _____

2. soften
   should'nt
   reduction
   misplaced
   _____

3. invention
   weight
   graphicly
   interesting
   _____

4. trophys
   stepping
   restriction
   committee
   _____

5. cheif
   activate
   vision
   extent
   _____

6. translate
   stretchs
   falsehood
   delightful
   _____

7. scenic
   guiding
   lighten
   feetured
   _____

8. unknown
   prospective
   preformer
   maintain
   _____

E

Each sentence has one misspelled word.
Write each word correctly on the blank.

1. His usualy composed wife was very discouraged. _____

2. Cut the loafes in half with that knife. _____

3. Motherhood requires contientous and often
   physical work. _____

Lesson 87

_ _ _ _ _ _   _ _ p _ o a _ _   _ _   _ c q _ _ _ _ _ _

_ _   w l e _ _ _   _ _ s c _ _ _ _ _ _   _ _.

_____

_____

B

1. _____

_____

2. _____

_____

C

1. _____   4. _____

2. _____   5. _____

3. _____   6. _____

D

Add the morphographs together.
Remember to use the rule about adding **al** before **ly.**

1. proper + ly   = _____

2. base + ic + ly   = _____

3. physic + ly   = _____

4. order + ly   = _____

5. hero + ic + ly   = _____

6. un + like + ly   = _____

7. comic + ly   = _____

Fill in the blanks to show the morphographs in each word.

1. _____ + _____ + _____ = belongs

2. _____ + _____ + _____ = designate

3. _____ + _____ + _____ = replied

4. _____ + _____ + _____ = confusing

5. _____ + _____ = transmit

6. _____ + _____ + _____ = avoiding

7. _____ + _____ + _____ = describing

8. _____ + _____ + _____ = invention

9. _____ + _____ + _____ + _____ = activation

10. _____ + _____ + _____ = likelihood

11. _____ + _____ + _____ = proposal

12. _____ + _____ + _____ = objective

Each sentence has one misspelled word.
Write each word correctly on the blank.

1. The bare discovered some wild berries. _____

2. My friend doesn't usually permitt me to use her skates. _____

3. The commisioner obtained permission to reduce our taxes. _____

A

1. _____

_____

2. _____

_____

B

1. _____   5. _____

2. _____   6. _____

3. _____   7. _____

4. _____   8. _____

C

Dear Pat,

Thank you vary much for the pet lizard you sent me. Wood you believe that the little fellow has begun snaping at people? My aunt was playing with him last nite. Suddenly the lizard jumped up and bit her write on the nose. Luckyly the bite wasn't bad.

I'm sending you a photograf of the lizard sleeping with our cat. Those too have become like bruthers.

Thanks again for the unuseual pet.

Your freind,

Chris

_____

_____

_____

_____

_____

_____

_____

_____

D

Write **s** or **es** in the second column.
Then add the morphographs together.

1. apply + _____ = _____

2. reach + _____ = _____

3. duty + _____ = _____

4. press + _____ = _____

5. speak + _____ = _____

6. match + _____ = _____

7. stay + _____ = _____

8. rich + _____ = _____

E

Write the contractions for the words below.

1. they will = _____

2. who is = _____

3. can not = _____

4. we are = _____

5. they have = _____

6. would not = _____

Lesson 89

The <u>people</u> in the picture are very busy.

The man by the sink is <u>looking</u> at the clock.

He has only an <u>hour</u> to <u>finush</u> <u>washing</u> the <u>dishes</u>.

The sink is only <u>half</u> full, so the man is <u>runing</u> more <u>water</u>.

The girl has a <u>box</u> in her hand. She is going to <u>defrost</u> the freezer.

She has already <u>cleaned</u> the <u>shelves</u>.

The <u>boy</u> on the <u>right</u> is <u>wrapping</u> a <u>loaf</u> of bread he made.

He <u>cut</u> <u>some</u> of the bread with a <u>knife</u> and ate it.

Everyone is being <u>helpful</u>.

Lesson 90 is a test lesson.
There is no worksheet.

Lesson 91

A

1. _____

   _____

2. _____

   _____

B

1. _____
2. _____
3. _____
4. _____

5. _____
6. _____
7. _____
8. _____

C

Circle the short **cvc** morphographs.

1. low
2. mit
3. temper
4. got
5. bug
6. fer
7. ply
8. fox
9. stop
10. get
11. pel
12. miss
13. cur
14. proper

Make twelve real words from the morphographs in the box.

| struct | verse | in | con | tent | vent | ion |

1. _____

2. _____

3. _____

4. _____

5. _____

6. _____

7. _____

8. _____

9. _____

10. _____

11. _____

12. _____

Lesson 92

A

Adequately protecting the environment is a challenge.

_____

_____

B

Add the morphographs together.

1. im + prove + ment = _____

2. e + value + ate = _____

3. be + lief + s = _____

4. ob + serve + ate + ion = _____

5. de + com + press + ion = _____

6. e + vent + ual = _____

7. con + vert + ed = _____

8. sign + ate + ure = _____

C

Draw a line from each word to its clue.

bare •   • what you wear

close •   • not covered

bear •   • Have you _____ my gloves?

clothes •   • I lost _____ by exercising.

seen •   • You must push the door hard to _____ it.

scene •   • Let's _____ for the others before we leave.

wait •   • an animal

weight •   • The peaceful _____ was interrupted by noisy campers.

These words are in the puzzle.
Circle six or more of the words.

today	draw	duty
tough	false	agree
over	grief	after
style		

t	o	u	g	h	s
a	o	v	e	r	t
f	g	d	u	t	y
t	r	r	a	l	l
e	i	a	e	y	e
r	e	w	g	e	e
d	f	a	l	s	e

Each sentence has one misspelled word.
Write each word correctly on the blank.

1. Scientists proclame that the new medication will
   improve the condition.   _____

2. The childhood belief in elves still fasinates many
   writers.   _____

3. The endless search for my beautiful bracelet was
   depresing.   _____

Lesson 93

A

permit   rob   perform   spot   transfer   recur

B

_ _ e q _ a _ _ _ _   _ _ _ _ _ _ _ _ _

_ _ _ _ _ _ r o n _ _ _ _ _ _ _ _ _

_ _ _ _ _ l e n g _ .

C

1. _____   5. _____

2. _____   6. _____

3. _____   7. _____

4. _____   8. _____

D

Write the plural for each word.
Remember to say the plural word to yourself.

1. life _____

2. wolf _____

3. knife _____

4. thief _____

5. elf _____

6. leaf _____

7. half _____

8. shelf _____

Fill in the blanks to show the morphographs in each word.

1. _____ + _____ + _____ = incurable

2. _____ + _____ + _____ = signature

3. _____ + _____ + _____ = perfection

4. _____ + _____ + _____ = disbelief

5. _____ + _____ + _____ = subtraction

6. _____ + _____ + _____ = improvement

7. _____ + _____ + _____ = textured

8. _____ + _____ + _____ = befriended

9. _____ + _____ + _____ = avoided

10. _____ + _____ + _____ + _____ = conversation

11. _____ + _____ + _____ = observer

12. _____ + _____ + _____ + _____ = transportation

Lesson 94

A

transmit   prefer   strain   hot

B

1. _____

_____

2. _____

_____

C

D

Write the plural for each word.
Some of the words have **ves** in the plural. Some don't, so be careful.

1. wolf _____
2. cliff _____
3. chief _____
4. wife _____

5. gulf _____
6. roof _____
7. life _____
8. calf _____

Choose one or more words from the list to complete each sentence.

hole   **write**   **week**   **whole**   **weak**   **right**

1. Jill visits her grandparents every month. Carlos visits his

   every _____.

2. Jim ate the _____ pie, and now he is sick.

3. I must remember to _____ a thank-you letter to my aunt.

4. Next _____ is Kim's birthday party. Are you going?

5. Margot is only four years old, but she already knows how to read

   and _____.

6. That beam is _____ because it has a _____ in it.

Lesson 95 is a test lesson.
There is no worksheet.

Lesson 96

commit   propel   reform   ship

Lesson 97

compel   stop   adjust   refer

1. _____   4. _____

2. _____   5. _____

3. _____   6. _____

Dear Customer:

    Are you spending more time than you need to on jobs arround the house? I am righting to inform you that we are now produsing the most usefull tool ever made for the home. The new E-Z Tool can do thousans of jobs in your home. It makes beds. It replases lightbulbs. It waters plants. It washs windows, serves your dinner, and cures bad breth, to. It comes packed in reuseable boxes. The E-Z Tool can easly be put together using instrucshuns that come with each order.

    Please send us your order tomorow.

Sincerely,

I. M. Selling

_____

_____

_____

_____

_____

_____

_____

_____

_____

_____

D

Fill in the blanks to show the morphographs in each word.

1. _____ + _____ = deceive

2. _____ + _____ + _____ = adjustment

3. _____ + _____ + _____ = emerged

4. _____ + _____ + _____ + _____ = observation

5. _____ + _____ + _____ = destruction

6. _____ + _____ + _____ = implied

E

Each sentence has one misspelled word.
Write each word correctly on the blank.

1. The robber avoided having a conversaion with
the detective.   _____

2. Protecting the enviroment will save many lives. _____

3. The king and his cheifs had an extended
conversation.   _____

Lesson 98

A

transmit   rerun   constrain   unstop

B

1. _____ + _____ + _____ = relentless

2. _____ + _____ + _____ = incomplete

3. _____ + _____ = surround

C

1. _____ + _____ = _____

2. _____ + _____ = _____

3. _____ + _____ = _____

4. _____ + _____ = _____

5. _____ + _____ = _____

6. _____ + _____ = _____

D

Add the morphographs together.

1. e + duce + ate = _____
2. ad + vent + ure + ous = _____
3. con + temple + ate = _____
4. ad + miss + ion = _____
5. com + plete + ly = _____
6. de + vast + ate + ing = _____
7. con + sume + er = _____
8. sup + ply + es = _____
9. sur + face = _____
10. ad + dress = _____

E

Write the plural for each word.
Some of the words have **ves** in the plural.
Some don't, so be careful.

1. photograph _____
2. cliff _____
3. leaf _____
4. shelf _____
5. calf _____
6. roof _____
7. wife _____
8. wolf _____

Lesson 99

A

repel   rob   subvert   outfit

B

1. _____

_____

2. _____

_____

C

1. _____   4. _____

2. _____   5. _____

3. _____   6. _____

D

Add the morphographs together.

1. re + late + ion + ship   = _____

2. in + stant + ly   = _____

3. sur + face   = _____

4. sup + ply + es   = _____

5. re + sume + ing   = _____

6. ad + miss + ion   = _____

7. e + vent + ful   = _____

8. im + per + fect   = _____

9. con + verse + ate + ion   = _____

10. fright + en + ing   = _____

E

Cross out the misspelled words in these sentences.
Then write the words correctly above the crossed-out words.

The scientest was fasinated by his own invention.

Do we need perrmission to copy this report?

The new close I bougth do'nt fit very well.

The comittee on conservation is interested in preserving the enviroment.

F

Each sentence has one misspelled word.
Write each word correctly on the blank.

1. The rich and famous will pay any prise for fashion. _____

2. She started crying suddenley, but her tears couldn't be explained. _____

3. We through balls with the children to help them be more active. _____

Lesson 100 is a test lesson.
There is no worksheet.

Lesson 101

The champion became a prominent citizen.

Lesson 102

A

character   family   trouble   brought

B

___ _h___ io_ __ca_e

_ _____i_e__ c__ize_.

_____

_____

C

1. _____   5. _____

2. _____   6. _____

3. _____   7. _____

4. _____   8. _____

Add the morphographs together.

1. de + tect + ion   = _____

2. inter + view + ed   = _____

3. pro + tect + ion   = _____

4. re + act + ion   = _____

5. in + vent + ion   = _____

6. trans + gress + ion = _____

7. fact + ion + s   = _____

8. con + tract + ion   = _____

9. sup + pose + ed   = _____

10. de + fect + ion   = _____

11. vise + ion   = _____

12. de + press + ion   = _____

These words are in the puzzle.
Circle seven or more of the words.

supply	worth	style
court	rope	speak
out	believe	keeper
relate	state	soon

c	r	u	p	p	b	s
s	o	o	n	l	e	t
w	s	u	p	p	l	y
o	p	t	r	e	i	l
r	e	l	a	t	e	e
t	a	a	l	t	v	e
h	k	e	e	p	e	r

Lesson 103

	ion form?	**or** or **er** form?
1. fact	_____	_____
2. design	_____	_____
3. invent	_____	_____
4. act	_____	_____
5. speak	_____	_____
6. photograph	_____	_____

B

_ _ _   _ _ _ _ _ _ o n _ _ a _ _

_   _ _ _ _ _ e _ _ _ _ _ _ z e _ .

_____

_____

C

rob   repel   subvert   cut

D

Circle the misspelled word in each group.
Then write it correctly on the line.

1. character	**2.** pitiful	**3.** fashion	**4.** unknowen
replyed	worthless	thieves	basically
project	danjerous	resonable	brought
subtract	rhythm	magically	science

_____   _____   _____   _____

E

Circle the short **cvc** morphographs.

1. snap   **3.** mark   **5.** pel   **7.** critic   **9.** ceive

2. fer   **4.** ship   **6.** mit   **8.** cur   **10.** box

F

Add the morphographs together.

1. e + duce + ate   = _____

2. inter + act + ion   = _____

3. sup + press + ion   = _____

4. e + mote + ion + al = _____

5. family + es   = _____

6. trouble + ing   = _____

Lesson 104

A

	ion form?	**or** or **er** form?
1. transgress	_____	_____
2. plant	_____	_____
3. project	_____	_____
4. compress	_____	_____
5. retain	_____	_____
6. tract	_____	_____

B

1. _____

_____

2. _____

_____

C

Add the morphographs together.

1. rerun + ing   = _____
2. refer + ing   = _____
3. hot + est   = _____
4. disarm + ed   = _____
5. commit + ed   = _____
6. ship + ing   = _____
7. detect + ive   = _____
8. snap + y   = _____

D

Make twelve real words from the morphographs in the box.

| ex | ion | com | press | re | sup | im | ive | de |

1. _____   7. _____

2. _____   8. _____

3. _____   9. _____

4. _____   10. _____

5. _____   11. _____

6. _____   12. _____

E

Each sentence has one misspelled word.
Write each word correctly on the blank.

1. Describing the robber's voise to the detective was _____ a challenge.

2. The flawwed signature was a trick to deceive my _____ assistant.

3. To adequeately evaluate the foxes, we will have to _____ encourage observation.

Lesson 105 is a test lesson.
There is no worksheet.

Lesson 106

A

1. _____   5. _____

2. _____   6. _____

3. _____   7. _____

4. _____   8. _____

B

Underline the morphograph that each word ends with.
Then add the next morphograph.

1. admit + ed   = _____

2. compel + ing = _____

3. expel + ed   = _____

4. instruct + ive = _____

5. protect + ion = _____

6. big + est   = _____

7. forgot + en = _____

8. recur + ing = _____

C

	ion form?	**or** or **er** form?
1. dictate	_____	_____
2. consume	_____	_____
3. invent	_____	_____
4. instruct	_____	_____
5. stretch	_____	_____
6. contract	_____	_____

D

1. _____ + _____ = profess

2. _____ + _____ = provide

E

Fill in the blanks to show the morphographs in each word.

1. _____ + _____ + _____ = medication

2. _____ + _____ + _____ = prediction

3. _____ + _____ = promote

4. _____ + _____ + _____ + _____ = emotional

5. _____ + _____ + _____ = confession

6. _____ + _____ = traction

7. _____ + _____ + _____ = attractive

8. _____ + _____ = interview

9. _____ + _____ + _____ = intersection

10. _____ + _____ + _____ = instantly

F

Each sentence has one misspelled word.
Write each word correctly on the blank.

1. The actor became emotional when he was
   interveiwed by a prominent photographer.   _____

2. To our disbelief, the supplies were shipped to a
   dishonist commissioner.   _____

3. The men avoided the vast cliffs because they were _____
   too much of a challange.

Lesson 107

A

1. _____

_____

2. _____

_____

B

Underline the morphograph that each word ends with.
Then add the next morphograph.

1. repel + ing = _____

2. remote + ly = _____

3. submit + ing = _____

4. commit + ment = _____

5. spot + less = _____

6. prefer + ed = _____

C

If there is an **i-o-n** form of the word, write it in the second column.
If there is no **i-o-n** form, leave the second column blank.
In the last column, write the word with the morphograph **o-r** or **e-r**.

	ion form?	**or** or **er** form?
1. heavy	_____	_____
2. vise	_____	_____
3. invent	_____	_____
4. misspell	_____	_____
5. profess	_____	_____

1. _____ + _____ = inquire

2. _____ + _____ = resemble

E

Complete each sentence correctly with one of these words.

week	piece	desert	weight	weak
bare	bear	wait	peace	dessert

1. Marty felt _____ all during his illness.

2. We go to school five days out of each _____.

3. Fighters used to box with their _____ hands.

4. We will _____ for you after school.

5. A _____ of wood broke off the chair.

6. I would never _____ a friend in trouble.

7. When I eat too much _____, I gain _____.

> There is no worksheet
> for Lesson 108.

Lesson 109

Several foreign nations considered the problem.

_____

_____

B

1. _____   5. _____

2. _____   6. _____

3. _____   7. _____

4. _____   8. _____

C

If there is an **i-o-n** form of the word, write it in the second column.
If there is no **i-o-n** form, leave the second column blank.
In the last column, write the word with the morphograph **o-r** or **e-r.**

	ion form?	**or** or **er** form?
1. educate	_____	_____
2. consume	_____	_____
3. conduct	_____	_____
4. invent	_____	_____
5. write	_____	_____
6. act	_____	_____

D

Write the correct spelling for each word.
Then write one of these letters after each number.

Write **O** if the word is spelled by just putting the morphographs together.
Write **A** if the final-**e** rule explains why the spelling is changed.
Write **B** if the doubling rule explains why the spelling is changed.
Write **C** if the **y**-to-**i** rule explains why the spelling is changed.

1. _____ re + ply + ed   = _____

2. _____ con + fuse + ion   = _____

3. _____ chance + y   = _____

4. _____ worth + y + ness   = _____

5. _____ grip + ed   = _____

6. _____ for + give + en   = _____

7. _____ study + ing   = _____

8. _____ storm + y + est   = _____

9. _____ re + serve + ate + ion = _____

10. _____ shop + er   = _____

11. _____ un + hurry + ed   = _____

12. _____ settle + ment   = _____

E

Circle the misspelled word in each group. Then write it correctly on the line.

1. copying	2. medical	3. wern't	4. unhappy
approve	perscription	puppies	delightful
beleive	maddest	source	famous
forgot	immobile	remark	tommorrow

_____   _____   _____   _____

Lesson 110 is a test lesson.
There is no worksheet.

158 Lesson 109

Lesson 111

A

_ _ _ e _ _ _   _ _ e i g _ _ _ _ _ _ _ _
_ _ s _ _ _ _ _   _ _ _ _ _ _ _ e _.

_____

_____

B

1. _____

_____

2. _____

_____

C

April 1

Dear Terry,

   Last weak my famly went to visit relutives. We had a wonderful time.

   I had my photograph taken with a fameous scientest. My cousin and I dug a whole in the woods and found a hiden treasure. Now we are vary rich. Someone gave my sister a valueable automobile. Later we won a radio contest. The prize was a trip arround the world. On the way home, we caught a theif who was robing a store.

   April Fool's Day!

Sincerely,

Robin

_____

_____

_____

_____

_____

_____

_____

_____

_____

Underline the morphograph that each word ends with.
Then add the next morphograph.

1. compel + ing   = _____

2. commit + ment = _____

3. report + er   = _____

4. permit + ed   = _____

5. prefer + ed   = _____

6. recap + ing   = _____

7. predict + ion   = _____

8. recur + ing   = _____

Fill in the blanks to show the morphographs in each word.

1. _____ + _____ + _____ = confession

2. _____ + _____ + _____ = designer

3. _____ + _____ + _____ + _____ = resignation

4. _____ + _____ + _____ = promotion

5. _____ + _____ + _____ = divided

6. _____ + _____ + _____ = attractive

7. _____ + _____ + _____ + _____ = information

8. _____ + _____ + _____ = adventure

Lesson 112

A

1. _____

_____

2. _____

_____

B

1. _____   4. _____

2. _____   5. _____

3. _____

C

If there is an **i-o-n** form of the word, write it in the second column.

If there is no **i-o-n** form, leave the second column blank.

In the last column, write the word with the morphograph **o-r** or **e-r.**

	ion form?	**or** or **er** form?
1. interview	_____	_____
2. instruct	_____	_____
3. contract	_____	_____
4. receive	_____	_____
5. invent	_____	_____
6. inspect	_____	_____

E

Make eight real words from the morphographs in the box.

verse	con	sign	re	sere	ion	ate

1. _____ 5. _____

2. _____ 6. _____

3. _____ 7. _____

4. _____ 8. _____

Lesson 113

A

1. _____   5. _____

2. _____   6. _____

3. _____   7. _____

4. _____   8. _____

B

bound   prime   custom   legend   cave   grave   ready   scarce

C

Lesson 114

A

1. _____

_____

2. _____

_____

B

1. _____   **4.** _____

2. _____   **5.** _____

3. _____

C

Underline the morphograph that each word ends with.
Then add the next morphograph.

1. permit + ed   = _____

2. unstop + able = _____

3. spin + ing   = _____

4. recur + ed   = _____

5. propel + er   = _____

6. invent + ive = _____

D

Add the morphographs together.

1. re + quire + ment + s = _____

2. in + di + vide + ual = _____

3. de + cise + ion + s = _____

4. pro + fess + ion + al = _____

5. tempt + ate + ion = _____

6. at + tent + ion = _____

7. re + mote + ly = _____

8. mote + ive + ate = _____

9. di + strict = _____

10. un + sur + pass + ed = _____

E

Fill in the circle marked **R** if the underlined word is spelled right.
Fill in the circle marked **W** if the underlined word is spelled wrong.

1. We ate fresh fruit for <u>desert</u>.   Ⓡ   Ⓦ

2. The study of insects <u>fascinates</u> me.   Ⓡ   Ⓦ

3. Jake's mother works for the <u>goverment</u>.   Ⓡ   Ⓦ

4. Our friends <u>bougth</u> a new automobile.   Ⓡ   Ⓦ

5. Some forms of energy are <u>destructive</u> to the environment.   Ⓡ   Ⓦ

6. My doctor won't write a <u>persription</u> unless it is really necessary.   Ⓡ   Ⓦ

Lesson 115 is a test lesson.
There is no worksheet.

Lesson 116

A

It's probably not necessary to continue the competition.

_____

_____

B

1. _____   5. _____

2. _____   6. _____

3. _____   7. _____

4. _____   8. _____

C

If there is an **i-o-n** form of the word, write it in the second column.
If there is no **i-o-n** form, leave the second column blank.
In the last column, write the word with the morphograph **o-r** or **e-r**.

	ion form?	**or** or **er** form?
1. vise	_____	_____
2. profess	_____	_____
3. review	_____	_____
4. contract	_____	_____
5. perform	_____	_____
6. protect	_____	_____

D

Add the morphographs together.
Remember to use your rule about adding **en**.

1. know + en = _____

2. tough + en = _____

3. draw + en = _____

4. sew + en = _____

5. grow + en = _____

6. prove + en = _____

E

Fill in the blanks to show the morphographs in each word.

1. _____ + _____ + _____ = precisely

2. _____ + _____ = require

3. _____ + _____ + _____ = inquiry

4. _____ + _____ + _____ = commotion

5. _____ + _____ + _____ = remoteness

6. _____ + _____ + _____ = attraction

7. _____ + _____ + _____ + _____ = relationship

8. _____ + _____ + _____ = supplied

Lesson 117

A

___' ___ b a b __ ___
__ c _ s s a __ __ _____ u e ___
____ e __ t ___.

_____

_____

B

1. _____

_____

2. _____

_____

C

Draw a line from each word to its clue.

dessert •   • My parents were _____ in a small town.

barely •   • The tourists had a _____ view of the mountain.

married •   • We _____ finished the assignment.

weight •   • Have you _____ the new invention?

scenic •   • something you eat

desert •   • We changed our _____ after school.

seen •   • Pat lost _____ by exercising.

clothes •   • to leave

D

Add the morphographs together.
Remember to use the rule about adding **al** before **ly.**

1. critic + ly = _____

2. graph + ic + ly = _____

3. de + light + ful + ly = _____

4. physic + ly = _____

5. real + ly = _____

6. base + ic + ly = _____

7. comic + ly = _____

8. un + like + ly = _____

E

Add the morphographs together.

1. pro + fess + ion + al = _____

2. di + stress + ing = _____

3. re + sume + ed = _____

4. ex + plore + ate + ion = _____

5. dis + courage + ment = _____

6. dis + sect = _____

7. con + front + ate + ion = _____

8. im + proper + ly = _____

Lesson 118

A

1. _____

_____

2. _____

_____

B

1. _____   4. _____

2. _____   5. _____

3. _____

C

1. _____ + _____ = record

2. _____ + _____ + _____ = dictionary

D

Write the plural for each word.

1. worry _____

2. thief _____

3. scratch _____

4. chief _____

5. wife _____

6. bush _____

7. study _____

8. leaf _____

9. view _____

10. copy _____

E

Underline the morphograph that each word ends with.
Then add the next morphograph.

1. forget + ing = _____

2. compel + ed = _____

3. inspect + ion = _____

4. dog + y = _____

5. transfer + ed = _____

6. contain + er = _____

F

Each sentence has one misspelled word.
Write each word correctly on the blank.

1. To the relief of the students, the strict professer
   was dismissed. _____

2. Sevral nations provide protection to foreign citizens. _____

3. The gradual increase in temperature this week
   improoved everyone's mood. _____

4. The photagraphs of the island were remarkable. _____

A

B

Circle the short **cvc** morphographs.

1. water
2. fer
3. rent
4. poison

5. big
6. spirit
7. stay
8. cur

9. motor
10. pel
11. critic
12. box

13. mit
14. wander
15. low
16. flat

C

Fill in the blanks to show the morphographs in each word.

1. _____ + _____ + _____ = dictionary
2. _____ + _____ + _____ + _____ = unrecorded
3. _____ + _____ + _____ = partially
4. _____ + _____ + _____ = precisely
5. _____ + _____ = married
6. _____ + _____ + _____ + _____ = preservation

D

Each sentence has one misspelled word.
Write each word correctly on the blank.

1. The reportor instantly knew that the information would _____ be scarce.

2. We permited the writer to use her notes. _____

3. According to an old ledgand, the cave was the home _____ of a frightening animal.

Lesson 120 is a test lesson.
This is the last worksheet in Level E.

Word List

Word List

Word List

word	lesson	word	lesson	word	lesson	word	lesson	word	lesson
hopping	11	insects	106	I've	41	liked	9	magically	71
hottest	39	insist	68	jacket	96	likelihood	77	main	107
hour	89	insisted	69	jar	52	likely	74	maintain	33
house	12	inspect	34	joy	13	likeness	6	major	2
hurried	21	inspection	34	joyous	27	likes	11	making	52
hurries	38	inspector	112	joyously	36	lilies	66	many	3
hurry	66	instance	117	joys	31	line	101	married	117
hurrying	57	instant	99	judge	12	listen	4	marry	108
image	83	instantly	99	keeper	102	listening	89	massive	23
immobile	82	instead	19	kick	36	little	4	match	1
immovable	99	instruct	64	kind	9	live	12	matches	26
impart	87	instruction	66	kindest	44	livelihood	87	matchless	1
imperfect	79	instructional	73	kindly	44	liveliness	68	maybe	4
implied	97	instructions	97	kindness	6	lives	79	meat	18
imply	86	instructive	106	kings	21	loaf	76	medic	54
import	87	instructor	103	knife	77	loan	8	medical	73
imported	94	intend	62	knives	81	loaves	79	medicate	82
improperly	94	intensive	51	know	43	lock	89	medication	86
improve	87	intensively	48	knowledge	86	lodge	38	meet	18
improved	93	intent	91	known	61	logic	4	meets	56
improvement	88	intention	37	large	34	logically	71	merge	61
inborn	18	intentional	63	largely	39	lone	8	merged	69
incision	108	interaction	103	largest	16	loneliest	34	merry	112
incomplete	98	intercept	101	last	4	lonely	16	misconception	28
increase	19	interested	13	latch	33	look	37	misfile	2
increases	47	interesting	39	lately	24	looking	89	misfiles	11
increasing	21	intermission	101	leaf	77	loose	11	mishandle	1
increasingly	38	intersect	102	learn	86	loosely	17	misinformed	54
incur	74	intersection	106	leave	4	loosen	16	misjudge	1
incurable	93	interview	101	leaves	78	lose	3	mismatch	1
individual	114	interviewed	102	ledge	37	losses	54	misplace	2
infect	72	interviewer	112	legend	113	louder	31	misplaced	44
infection	74	invaluable	26	length	4	low	22	misprint	1
inflamed	51	invent	57	lengthen	18	lower	26	misquote	4
information	111	invented	58	let's	36	lowest	23	misreported	19
informative	82	invention	57	life	77	luckiest	52	misshape	4
informed	19	inventive	72	lifeless	13	luckily	36	misshapen	41
informer	18	inventor	103	light	18	lucky	21	mission	67
inhuman	18	inverse	91	lighten	46	mad	9	misspell	3
injected	29	inversion	91	lighter	13	madder	17	misspeller	107
injection	27	invert	88	lightest	46	maddest	17	misspelling	8
inland	18	inverted	93	lightly	46	made	52	mist	1
inquire	107	island	48	lights	21	madly	17	mistake	67
inquiry	116	its	52	likable	6	madness	14	mistaken	36
insect	102	it's	49	like	3	magic	47	misuse	2

Word List

Word List

quotable 6	refer 51	requesting........41	revert 88	sale 51
quote 4	referring 97	require 116	review 7	saltiest 83
racial 118	refillable 7	requirement ...114	reviewed 46	salty 21
racist..................39	refine................62	requirements..114	reviewer 46	saw 78
raging 13	refined................16	rerunning 98	reviewing 46	saying 17
rainiest 61	reform 62	resemble........107	revise 41	scales 113
range 37	reformed 96	resented...........41	revised 81	scar 9
rather 19	refreshing 8	reservation.....109	revision 43	scarce............113
ration 23	refusal...............31	reserve..............6	rhythm 58	scariest 51
reach 33	refuse................82	reserved............21	rhythmic............61	scary 88
reaches.............28	refused...............62	resign 47	rhythmical.........64	scene...............59
reacting.............26	regard 43	resignation.....111	rhythmically 73	scenic 67
reaction............27	regardless 48	resigned............69	rich 9	scenically 72
reactor 104	regress 26	resist 68	riches 27	science 1
read 12	regressing 4	resisted 73	ridge 36	scientist 66
readily 54	reinstate 19	resolve 36	right 8	scientists 61
readiness 46	reject.................27	resolved 42	rights 38	scope................64
ready...................41	rejecting............26	resource 7	ripen 61	scratch..............36
real.....................66	rejection 28	resourceful.........4	ripeness 17	scratches........118
realistic 52	relate 4	respectable......42	ripening 42	scribe................9
really 14	relation..............41	respectful.........34	riper 17	script..................14
reappear 86	relationship 99	respectfully 69	ripest 11	scripts...............27
reason................1	relative 27	rest....................44	river...................113	scripture 31
reasonable.........3	relatives 111	restful...................2	robber 93	sculpture..........56
reasoning.........11	relentless 98	restfully 19	robbing 103	search...............34
rebuild..............43	relief 91	resting...............44	rocks 19	searches 36
recapping 111	relieve 92	restless 1	roofs 94	seed.................64
receive 94	remarkable.........6	restlessness........7	rope 102	seeds................89
receiver...........112	remotely.........107	restoring 9	round 28	seek.................12
reception 26	remoteness....116	restrain..............4	roundly 74	seen.................62
receptive 24	removal..............39	restrict 36	ruling................12	seize 28
record 118	remove..............4	restriction.........44	run 8	seizure 28
recover................6	rental................12	resume..............97	runner 36	self...................77
recovered.........42	repel.................39	resumed.........117	running 21	selves 81
recreation.........48	repelling 99	resuming...........99	runny.................26	serve..................3
recur 74	replace 4	retain................33	sad.....................46	serving..............7
recurred 114	replaces 97	retained...........67	sadden............14	settle.................21
recurring 93	replacing 8	retainer 104	sadder 46	settlement........23
rediscover........42	replied..............86	retention 59	saddest 12	several 109
rediscovered....42	reply.................86	return..................4	sadly 92	sew 56
redissolve 42	report 6	returnable 4	sadness 11	sewn 61
reduce 44	reporter...........111	returning 7	safest 17	shake 64
reduced 56	repressive 24	reusable 97	sail 56	shame.............61
reducing............43	request 19	reversal 61	saint..................68	shamefully 63
reduction 46	requested 48	reverse 68	saintly 69	shameless 9

Word List

word	lesson	word	lesson	word	lesson	word	lesson	word	lesson
shelf	76	slipped	12	stack	37	studious	29	tear	119
she'll	49	slipping	17	stage	38	studiously	37	temper	83
shelves	79	smiling	11	staging	7	studying	18	temperature	94
shine	78	snapped	13	stance	117	sturdiness	18	temple	81
shiniest	34	snapping	88	star	8	style	34	tempt	83
shining	83	snappy	104	starless	11	stylish	44	temptation	114
shipped	96	sneak	4	starred	18	stylishly	44	tend	78
shipping	104	sneaky	89	starring	13	subject	64	tense	17
shoes	96	snuggest	17	state	17	submerge	64	tension	23
shop	52	snugness	11	statement	22	submerged	73	tent	12
shopper	13	soften	53	station	41	submission	86	text	22
shops	12	softening	51	stay	14	submissive	77	texture	24
short	11	solve	7	stayed	19	submitting	107	textured	93
shortly	81	solved	42	stays	31	subscribe	64	thank	37
shouldn't	37	solving	8	stepped	13	subscription	67	that	67
show	56	some	4	stepping	12	subsist	68	that's	37
showed	52	soon	102	steps	21	substance	117	their	8
shown	61	sore	4	stopper	97	substantial	100	there	8
shrink	16	soreness	8	stopping	11	substantive	99	they	4
shrinkage	73	sort	78	storage	18	subtract	67	they'd	49
sign	9	sound	4	store	9	subtraction	68	they'll	36
signal	11	sounded	8	stored	11	subvert	88	they're	36
signature	82	source	3	stories	31	subverted	99	they've	37
silk	36	sow	53	stormiest	109	suddenly	99	thick	34
simple	41	speak	28	storminess	71	supplied	116	thicken	44
simplest	47	speaker	103	straight	21	supplier	108	thicker	44
simply	44	speaks	88	straighten	17	supplies	98	thickness	44
singing	7	speediest	38	strainer	94	supply	98	thief	42
sister	68	speedily	83	straining	7	support	98	thieves	78
sketch	34	speedy	21	strayed	22	supports	117	things	86
sketches	101	spelling	104	strength	11	suppose	98	think	38
skidded	83	spend	78	strengthen	36	supposed	102	thirst	22
skidding	13	spent	3	strengthening	39	suppression	103	thirsty	28
skillful	89	sphere	58	stress	38	surface	98	this	74
skills	19	spherical	52	stressful	51	surround	98	thorough	73
skin	9	spin	34	stretch	27	surrounded	102	thoroughly	83
skinned	68	spinner	41	stretcher	106	surroundings	108	those	28
sleep	61	spinning	14	stretches	27	swim	3	thought	1
sleepiness	74	spirit	22	strict	17	swimmer	13	thoughtful	2
sleepless	3	spiritual	76	strictly	19	tail	8	thoughtless	1
sleeplessness	61	spotless	12	structure	64	taking	16	thousand	64
sleepy	89	spotted	18	student	73	tale	8	thousands	97
sleeve	4	spotting	18	students	84	talked	114	threaten	62
slick	38	spotty	34	studied	21	taxes	27	three	96
slip	8	sprays	38	studies	31	teacher	13	threw	9

Study Lists

1-5

base
breakable
cover
cure
doubt
doubtful
fresh
guide
helpless
like
match
matchless
misfile
misjudge
mismatch
misplace
misquote
misshape
misspell
misuse
mother
move
name
painful
place
pointless
portable
power
powerful
powerless
price
print
quote
reason
reasonable
relate
remove
resourceful
restful
restrain
return
returnable

serve
sleepless
sore
sound
thought
thoughtless
view
workable
worth
worthless

6-10

athletes
breath
brightness
cheerful
curable
doubting
exercised
fair
fairness
faithful
fashion
fashionable
fearful
feat
feet
firmness
globe
guided
guiding
having
hear
helped
helplessness
here
hole
hopeless
hoping
kindness
likable
liked
likeness

loan
lone
misspelling
morning
named
nineteen
painfulness
peace
piece
priceless
pricing
quotable
recover
refillable
refreshing
remarkable
replace
replacing
report
reserve
resource
restlessness
restoring
returning
review
rich
right
scribe
serving
shameless
sign
singing
solve
solving
soreness
sounded
source
staging
store
straining
tail
tale
their
there

thoughtful
threw
through
throughout
timeless
to
too
traced
tribe
turned
uncover
unfair
unfairness
unhappy
used
useless
valuable
value
vary
very
weakness
weather
whether
whole
wood
would
write
youthfulness

11-15

biggest
coolest
darker
darkest
doubtless
dropper
farmer
final
finer
firm
flatly
flatness
formal

fresher
fright
frost
global
greatest
helper
hopeful
hopping
interested
length
lifeless
lighter
loose
madness
mothering
part
people
photograph
placing
planned
proving
quickly
raging
really
reasoning
rental
ripest
sadden
saddest
sadness
script
short
signal
skidding
slipped
smiling
snapped
snugness
spinning
spotless
starless
starring
stepped
stepping

Study Lists

stopping
stored
strength
swimmer
teacher
tone
tough
trapped
tribal
verse
wandering
weren't
widely
widest
winner
wonderful

16-20

anybody
ate
barred
boats
carried
carrying
change
claim
confine
conform
confronted
conserve
crease
creased
create
darken
defining
delight
delights
departed
deport
describe
drying
eight
fanciest

finely
finest
frightening
govern
happiness
healthy
helplessly
hiding
hoped
inborn
inhuman
inland
instead
largest
lonely
loosely
loosen
madder
madly
meat
meet
misreported
nastiest
package
peaceful
pitiful
pitying
playful
playing
press
quest
rather
refined
reinstate
restfully
ripeness
riper
rocks
safest
saying
shrink
skills
slipping
snuggest

spotted
spotting
starred
starring
state
storage
straighten
strict
studying
sturdiness
taking
tense
tighten
treat
tried
unconfirmed
unreformed
unresolvable
uselessness
using
which
worldly
worrier
wreckage

21-25

action
active
agree
cause
changing
clapping
confinement
context
crying
deforming
denial
detecting
easy
edgy
exchange
exchanging
explain

express
facing
feature
found
government
great
hurried
increasing
kings
lately
lights
lowest
lucky
massive
nastier
passion
passive
poisoned
portion
pressure
proclaim
proclaimed
profile
profound
progress
proudly
prove
proven
ration
receptive
repressive
reserved
running
salty
settle
settlement
speedy
spirit
statement
steps
straight
strayed
studied
tension

text
texture
thirst
toys
trapper
treatment
trial
varied
walls
worried

26-30

boxes
brushes
buzzes
claims
concept
conjecture
danger
defeated
dejected
depression
detect
detective
duty
except
expressed
expression
famous
featuring
fineness
fitness
flawed
furious
fury
glorious
happiest
happily
injected
injection
invaluable
joyous
lower

Study Lists

maddest
matches
misconception
movement
notion
passes
poisonous
preschool
preserve
presses
preview
profoundly
progressed
progression
progressive
project
protect
protection
protective
reaches
reaction
reception
regress
reject
rejecting
rejection
relative
riches
round
runny
seize
seizure
shops
speak
stretch
studious
taxes
thirsty
unexpected
waltzes
wash
wideness

31-35

actively
babies
beautiful
beauty
berries
black
boys
bridge
cage
carries
cities
contain
copies
count
cries
dangerous
deception
detain
detection
development
dress
duties
edginess
exception
flies
fork
friendliness
furiously
furry
hedge
inspect
inspection
joys
judge
large
latch
logic
loneliest
maintain
major
nice
noisily

order
park
physical
pinches
plays
pleasure
poisons
projecting
projection
prospect
questionable
reach
refusal
respectful
retain
science
scripture
search
shiniest
sketch
spin
spotty
stays
stories
studies
style
think
tour
tries
truck
trucks
type
union
worries

36-40

aren't
artist
batch
can't
catches
class
cloudiness

container
couldn't
dangerously
denies
disarm
discharged
discounts
discovering
disease
dislike
dispel
displeasing
ditch
doggy
don't
dresses
dries
easiest
exceptional
expel
force
forcefully
fuss
getting
glasses
gloriously
here's
hurries
increasingly
intention
joyously
kick
largely
ledge
let's
look
nervous
nervously
patch
placement
player
pledge
progressively
propel

range
removal
repel
ridge
scratch
searches
scientist
shouldn't
silk
speediest
sprays
stack
strengthening
stretches
studiously
thank
that's
they'll
they're
they've
think
tourist
trials
trick
unexpected
unions
varies
various
variously
voice
we'll
we're
who's

41-45

artistic
basic
beautifully
bought
brief
build
building
chance

Study Lists

chief
chiefly
childish
committee
conception
courage
creation
cross
crosses
deceptive
deduce
departure
descriptive
devise
didn't
discover
discovered
disrespect
dissolving
ditches
doesn't
foolish
graphic
grief
heavy
heroic
high
honesty
I've
kind
kindest
kindly
misplaced
misshapen
niece
photography
produce
produced
prospective
question
ready
rediscovered
reduce
reducing

regard
relation
requesting
resented
resolve
resolved
respectable
rest
resting
restless
restriction
revise
revision
ripening
simple
spinner
star
station
stylish
stylishly
thick
thicken
thicker
thickness
thief
typical
undiscovered
unrecovered
unresolved
unrevised
vision
we've

46-50

afternoon
boyish
classical
close
clothes
conduct
conducted
creative
designer

discourage
edging
evening
explorers
forceful
intensively
island
it's
magic
nieces
producing
product
productive
readiness
recreation
reduction
regardless
requested
resign
she'll
simplest
some
they'd
today
tomorrow
transaction
transform
transport
treasure
what's
yesterday
you'll

51-55

athletic
benches
bodies
cleanliness
comic
confer
conquests
critic
critical

defer
depose
deserve
design
discouragement
disgraceful
disorder
disposal
dispose
evenings
expose
finally
finish
finished
inflamed
intensive
losses
medic
misinformed
monkeys
pain
peacefully
prefer
prescribe
prescription
production
propose
provision
pulse
puppies
readily
realistic
refer
request
sale
scariest
soften
softening
sow /ō/
spherical
stressful
tragic
transcribe
transfer

transgression
translation
trays
trickiest
wishes

56-60

appoint
appraisal
appraise
approve
blow
chancy
comical
content
convention
cycle
draw
exposure
expressive
extent
grow
hurrying
invent
invention
know
prevent
proposal
reduced
retention
rhythm
sail
scene
sculpture
sew
show
sphere
throw
translated
typist
venture

Study Lists

61-65

accident
appointment
assistants
automobile
blown
construct
contend
contents
define
deform
description
destruction
disclosure
dishonest
disposable
drawn
easily
extend
extended
extension
forbid
forget
forgive
forgiven
golden
ground
grown
hottest
instruct
intend
intentional
known
merge
pretend
prevention
rainiest
refine
reform
reversal
rhythmic
rhythmical
ripen

scientists
seen
sewn
shame
shamefully
shopper
shown
sleep
sleeplessness
strengthen
structure
subject
submerge
subscribe
threaten
thrown
unintended
ventured
while

66-70

assistant
brother
carelessly
cheerfulness
consist
construction
contract
crashes
cubic
cyclist
extract
failure
false
falsely
flattest
forgetful
forgiving
foxes
friendliest
grounds
habit
insist

insisted
instruction
lengthen
lilies
liveliness
object
objective
observe
obtain
obtained
payment
peaches
perception
perform
pertain
ponies
pound
pretending
resigned
resist
respectfully
retained
reverse
saint
sister
skinned
subsist
subtract
subtraction
tightening
tract
traction
transplant
trophies
unbreakable
wakening
weight
worthy

71-75

aground
alike
along

apart
appears
around
athletically
awaken
basically
classically
comically
complain
compose
compress
compression
concur
conscientious
contentment
costly
critically
cubically
defective
delightful
distraction
extraction
firmly
graphically
heroically
incur
infect
infection
instructional
likely
logically
magically
nicely
objection
oblong
observer
observing
perceptive
perfect
perfection
performer
persisted
physically
recur

resisted
rhythmically
roundly
scenically
sleepiness
storminess
strictly
student
submerged
thorough
tragically
unapproved
wait

76-80

across
alone
apiece
bear
boyhood
calf
childhood
commission
commissioner
commit
compile
contraction
defrosting
destructive
dismiss
factual
falsehood
globally
gradual
habitual
half
halves
imperfect
knife
leaf
leaves
life
likelihood

Study Lists

loaf
loaves
mission
motherhood
objectionable
permission
permit
self
shelf
shelves
spiritual
submissive
thieves
transmission
transmit
usual
usually
wife
wives
wolf
wolves

81-85

activate
appear
avoidable
bare
calves
composure
confuse
confusion
conservation
defuse
designate
elves
ethically
explorer
friend
image
immobile
informative
knives
medicate

mobile
obstruction
please
proper
properly
pulsate
pure
refuse
revised
selves
shortly
signature
temper
temple
tempt
thoroughly
transfusion
vast
visual
void

86-90

acquiring
activation
applied
applies
apply
approach
avoiding
because
behave
belong
belongs
beside
casual
comply
confusing
contempt
convert
describing
devastating
fascinates
impart

imply
import
improve
invert
knowledge
livelihood
medication
observation
orderly
reappear
replied
reply
revert
speaks
submission
subvert
unlikely
weak

91-95

acquire
adequately
adjust
admit
advise
avoided
befriended
behaved
belief
beliefs
believable
believe
challenge
chiefs
cliffs
conceive
contention
convent
conversation
converse
conversion
converted
deceive

decompression
disbelief
eject
emerge
environment
evaluate
event
eventual
gulfs
imported
improperly
improved
improvement
incurable
intent
inverse
inversion
inverted
lives
perceive
permitting
preferred
protecting
receive
recurring
relief
robber
roofs
sadly
strainer
temperature
textured
transferring
transmitter
transportation
unusual
week

96-100

address
adjusted
adjustment
admission

adventure
committed
compelling
completely
constant
constrained
consume
consumer
contemplate
courtship
desert
educate
emerged
eventful
friendship
hardship
implied
incomplete
instant
instantly
opposed
outfitted
perfectly
photographs
presume
propeller
referring
reformed
relationship
relentless
repelling
rerunning
resume
resuming
shipped
stopper
substantial
substantive
supplies
supply
support
suppose
surface
surround

Study Lists

unstoppable

 101-105

actor
addictive
attain
attest
attract
became
brought
champion
character
citizen
composer
compressor
cutting
defection
defector
demote
dessert
dictate
disarmed
dissect
emotion
factions
factor
families
family
insect
instructor
interaction
intercept
intermission
intersect
interview
interviewed
inventor
motive
photographer
planter
predict
projector
prominent

promote
protector
reactor
retainer
robbing
shipping
snappy
speaker
subverted
supposed
suppression
surrounded
tractor
transgressor
trouble
troubling
unknown

106-110

admitted
attractive
commitment
concise
conduction
conductor
confession
considered
contractor
decisive
dictation
dictator
distant
divide
division
education
educator
expelled
foreign
forgotten
gripped
heavier
incision
inquire

instructive
intersection
marry
misspeller
nations
precise
prediction
problem
profess
profession
professor
promoter
promotion
provide
remotely
resemble
reservation
several
stormiest
submitting
unhurried
visor
worthiness
writer

111-115

attempt
attention
bound
cave
custom
decisions
district
divided
grave
individual
information
inspector
interviewer
inventive
legend
merry
motivate

permitted
prime
professional
promoted
recapping
recurred
reporter
requirement
requirements
resignation
scarce
temptation
unsurpassed

116-120

attraction
bushes
commotion
compelled
competition
confrontation
continue
delightfully
dictionary
distance
distressing
exploration
facial
forgetting
inquiry
instance
married
necessary
partial
partially
precisely
preservation
probably
racial
record
remoteness
require
resumed

reviewer
scratches
substance
supplied
toughen
transferred
unrecorded
views

Spelling Rules

Lesson	Rule	Explanation
6	**Final-E Rule**	When do you drop the final **e** from a word? When the next morphograph begins with a vowel letter.
11	**Doubling Rule (Short Words)**	When do you double the final **c** in a short word? When the word ends **cvc** and the next morphograph begins with **v.**
16	**Y-to-I Rule**	When do you change the **y** to **i** in a word? When the word ends with a consonant-and-**y** and the next morphograph begins with anything except **i.**
22	**W as a Vowel**	When is **w** a vowel letter? At the end of a morphograph.
23	**Y as a Vowel**	When is **y** a vowel letter? At the end of a morphograph.
26	**E-S Endings**	If a word ends in **s, z, sh,** or **ch,** you add **e-s** to make the plural word.
27	**E-S Endings** **X as Two Consonant Letters**	If a word ends in **x,** you add **e-s** to make the plural word. The letter **x** acts like two consonants because it has two consonant sounds.
31	**E-S Endings**	If a word ends with a consonant-and-**y,** you add **e-s** to make the plural word.
61	**E-N Variation**	If a word ends with the letter **w** and you add **e-n,** drop the **e.**
71	**A-L Insertion**	When a word ends in the letters **i-c,** you add the morphograph **a-l** before adding **l-y.**
78	**/ff/ Endings**	Some words that end in the sound **/ff/** have the letters **v-e-s** in the plural.
93	**Doubling Rule (Long Words)**	When the word ends in a short **cvc** morphograph, use the doubling rule.
103	**O-R Endings**	If a form of the word ends in **i-o-n,** use **o-r.**

Meanings of Affixes and Nonword Bases

Morphograph	Lesson	Meanings	Examples
a-	71	in, on, at; not, without	ahead; apart, atypical
-able	3	can be	stretchable, washable, readable
ad-	94	to, toward; against	advise, adjustment; adverse
-age	18	result of an action	package, usage, marriage
-al	12	related to, like	formal, trial, rental
ap-	56	to, toward, against	appointment, approval, appendage
-ary	118	related to; connected to	dictionary, library, secondary
at-	104	to, toward, against	attract, attention, attest
-ate	82	to make, act on; having the quality of	evaluate, activate; passionate
be-	86	to make; over; really	became, beside, because
ceive	94	to take; contain	receiver, conceive, deceived
cept	24	to take; contain	receptive, intercept, acceptable
cise	108	to cut	incision, concise, precisely
com-	73	with, together	compress, combat, commission
con-	19	with, together	conform, contest, condense
cord	118	rope; heart; in agreement	cording; record, accord, cordial
cur	74	to run, to happen	concur, recurred, current
de-	16	down, away from; reverse of; remove from	deport, deform, depart
di-	107	twice; through, across	divert, divide, direct
dict	104	to speak; to fix	predict, diction

Meanings of Affixes and Nonword Bases

Morphograph	Lesson	Meanings	Examples
dis-	37	opposite of; not; completely	dispel, discount, disease
duce	43	to lead	produce, educate, reducing
duct	46	to lead	productive, conductor, deductive
e-	92	missing out, away	eject, emitted, event
-ed	8	[action] in the past	formed, stepped, cried
-en	17	to make	loosen, darken, straighten
-er	13	more; one who	greater, lighter; teacher, dancer
-es	26	more than one; a verb marker for he, she, or it	lilies, boxes; watches, catches
-est	11	the most	greatest, lightest, happiest
ex-	21	out, away	export, exclude, extend
fect	72	to do, to make	defective, confection, perfect
fer	51	to carry	transfer, infer, referred
fess	106	to speak	profess, confession, professor
for-	63	against, completely	forbid, forgotten, forgiving
-ful	2	full of; tending to	careful, beautiful; forgetful
fuse	82	to pour or melt	transfusion, confusion
gress	24	to step	regression, progress, transgression
-hood	77	state, quality	motherhood, likelihood, childhood
-ial	118	related to, like	partial, facial, adverbial
-ic	43	like, related to	basic, typically, artistic

Meanings of Affixes and Nonword Bases

Morphograph	Lesson	Meanings	Examples
im-	87	in, into; not	impose, impression, impurity
in-	18	in, into; not; really	include; incurable; invaluable
-ing	7	when you do something, ongoing action	spending, moving, stopping
inter-	101	between	interact, intersect, intervention
-ion	23	state, quality, act, or process	action, taxation, repression
-ish	44	like, related to, inclined to be	babyish, stylish, boyish, greenish
-ist	39	one who	artist, typist, tourist
-ive	23	quality of; one who	expressive, informative; relative, detective
ject	26	to throw	rejecting, dejected, projection
-less	1	without	painless, useless, restless
lief	91	to lift, allow	belief, disbelief, relief
lieve	92	to lift, allow	believe, believable
-ly	14	how something is done	quietly, equally, basically
-ment	22	result of doing something	placement, requirement, apartment
mis-	1	wrongly	misspell, misjudge, misprint
miss	77	to send	admission, dismiss, missile
mit	78	to send	transmit, admitted, commitment
mote	103	to move	motionless, demote, promotional
-ness	6	that which is, quality of	thickness, quietness, freshness
ob-	67	to, toward, against	obstruct, obtain, objection

Meanings of Affixes and Nonword Bases

Morphograph	Lesson	Meanings	Examples
-ous	27	having the quality of	famous, furious, joyous
pel	39	to push	expel, propeller, repellent
per	69	through	perform, pertain, perceive
ply	86	a layer; to fold; full	pliable; comply; supplier
pose	54	to act a certain way; to put, to place	position, composure, opposite
pre-	26	before	preview, preclude, prepay
pro-	22	in favor of; before; forward	proclaim; provision; progress
quest	16	to seek, to ask for	conquest, request, questionable
quire	107	to seek, to ask for	inquire, requirement, acquire
re-	4	again, back	rerun, return, replace
-s	19	more than one; a verb marker for *he, she,* or *it*	friends, bananas, farmers; acts, writes, talks
sect	102	to cut	section, dissect, intersect
semble	107	same; together	resemble; assemble, ensemble
-ship	97	state, quality	friendship, hardship, relationship
sist	68	to stand, to set, to make	persist, resist, consists
spect	34	to look	inspect, respect, perspective
stance	117	to stand, to set	instance, substance, distance
stant	99	to stand, to set	constant, substantive, instant
struct	64	to build	structure, destruction, constructive
sub-	64	under	subtract, subhuman, submission

Meanings of Affixes and Nonword Bases

Morphograph	Lesson	Meanings	Examples
sume	97	to take	consumer, resume, presumable
sup-	98	under	support, suppressed, supposed
tain	33	to hold	retaining, container, detained
tect	24	to cover	detecting, protection
tend	62	to be inclined to; to stretch	attend, intend; extend
tent	59	to hold	content, attention, intent
tract	67	to drag, to draw	tractor, attractive, subtraction
trans-	49	across	transportation, transform, transfer
-ual	76	related to, like	factual, usual, gradual
un-	9	not, the opposite	unhappy, unusual, untie
-ure	24	act, process	departure, pressure, failure
vent	57	to come	prevent, invention, adventure
vert	88	to turn	invert, convert, introvert
vide	106	to see; to separate	providing; divide, individual
vise	41	to see; to separate	advise, visual; division
-y	21	having the quality of; belonging to	shiny, dreamy, mighty

Contractions

Component Words	Contractions	Component Words	Contractions
are not	aren't	should not	shouldn't
can not	can't	that is	that's
could not	couldn't	they are	they're
did not	didn't	they had	they'd
do not	don't	they have	they've
does not	doesn't	they will	they'll
have not	haven't	was not	wasn't
he had	he'd	we are	we're
he is	he's	we had	we'd
he will	he'll	we have	we've
here is	here's	we will	we'll
I am	I'm	were not	weren't
I have	I've	what is	what's
I will	I'll	who is	who's
it is	it's	would not	wouldn't
let us	let's	you are	you're
she had	she'd	you had	you'd
she is	she's	you will	you'll
she will	she'll		

Homonyms

ate   refers to: eat in the past
        example: I *ate* a sandwich.

eight   refers to: the number 8
        example: The dog had *eight* puppies.

bare   refers to: without covering; empty
        example: In the winter some trees are *bare.*

bear   refers to: a certain animal, or to support
        example: The huge *bear* drank from a stream.
        example: The bridge can't *bear* more weight.

close   refers to: shut something
        example: Please *close* the door.

clothes   refers to: things you wear
        example: They bought lots of *clothes.*

desert   refers to: leave or abandon
        example: I wouldn't *desert* a friend in need.

dessert   refers to: food served at the end of a meal
        example: We had ice cream for *dessert.*

feat   refers to: something hard to do
        example: Climbing the mountain was a great *feat.*

feet   refers to: body part
        example: Her *feet* were sore from running.

for   refers to: in place of
        example: She went to the store *for* me.

four   refers to: the number 4
        example: Cats have *four* legs.

hear   refers to: listen
        example: I can't *hear* you.

here   refers to: this place
        example: Come over *here.*

hole   refers to: empty space
        example: I have a *hole* in my sock.

whole   refers to: entire, complete
        example: He ate the *whole* pie.

loan   refers to: allow to borrow something
        example: She will *loan* me lunch money.

lone   refers to: by itself
        example: There was a *lone* tree.

marry   refers to: wed or unite
        example: She said she would *marry* Steve.

merry   refers to: happy, full of fun
        example: The hikers were a *merry* group.

meat   refers to: food from animals
        example: Some people don't eat *meat.*

meet   refers to: come together
        example: We agreed to *meet* next week.

no   refers to: negative answer
        example: *No,* I'm not going.

know   refers to: understand or be familiar with
        example: We *know* how to sail.

Homonyms

peace   refers to: calm; no war

example: I like *peace* and quiet.

piece   refers to: a part

example: I ate a *piece* of fruit.

---

plain   refers to: simple; ordinary

example: She wore a *plain* black dress.

plane   refers to: flat surface; air transportation

example: The *plane* landed safely.

---

right   refers to: correct; opposite of left

example: All my answers were *right*.

example: She wears a ring on her *right* hand.

write   refers to: put words on paper

example: You must *write* neatly.

---

sail   refers to: travel on water in a ship or a boat

example: We learned how to *sail* at camp.

sale   refers to: available to buy; an offer at a cheaper price

example: Our house is for *sale*. He bought the shoes on *sale*.

---

scene   refers to: view or setting

example: It was a painting of an ocean *scene*.

seen   refers to: see in the past

example: I have *seen* that picture.

---

sew   refers to: join with a needle and thread

example: He will *sew* a new button on his coat.

sow   refers to: plant seeds

example: Farmers *sow* their fields in the early spring.

---

tail   refers to: the back end

example: The dog chased his *tail*.

tale   refers to: a story

example: He told an interesting *tale*.

---

their   refers to: belonging to them

example: It is *their* house.

there   refers to: that place

example: Go over *there*.

they're   refers to: they are

example: I think *they're* ready.

---

threw   refers to: throw in the past

example: She *threw* the ball.

through   refers to: in one side and out the other

example: We went *through* the tunnel.

---

to   refers to: at or toward

example: She walked *to* school.

too   refers to: also

example: Why don't you come along, *too*?

two   refers to: the number 2

example: I ate *two* apples.

---

vary   refers to: change

example: His moods *vary* from day to day.

very   refers to: really, quite, especially

example: That story is *very* imaginative.

Homonyms

wait   refers to: delay; expect something

          example: We had to *wait* an hour for the bus.

weight refers to: heaviness

          example: He felt like he had the *weight* of the world on his shoulders.

---

wear   refers to: have clothes on your body

          example: What shall I *wear* today?

where refers to: what place

          example: *Where* do you want to go?

---

weather refers to: what it feels like out of doors

          example: Always wear a hat in cold *weather.*

whether refers to: if

          example: I don't care *whether* I go or not.

---

weak   refers to: the opposite of strong

          example: The wrestler felt *weak* after the match.

week   refers to: seven days

          example: We go on vacation next *week.*

---

wood   refers to: what trees are made of

          example: We need *wood* for the fire.

would   refers to: what might happen

          example: I *would* like to go to Paris.

---

your   refers to: belonging to you

          example: *Your* coat is blue.

you're refers to: you are

          example: *You're* early.

Short-Vowel, Long-Vowel Spelling Patterns

an   en   in   on   un

Part A	
badge	trudge
edge	page
hedge	rage
ledge	stage
pledge	wage
sledge	change
ridge	range
bridge	fringe
dodge	sponge
lodge	barge
budge	large
fudge	age
judge	cage
nudge	huge

Part B		
back	thick	dark
sack	shock	park
tack	rock	fork
stack	lock	desk
black	block	mask
track	knock	break
neck	clock	thank
deck	luck	cheek
speck	stuck	walk
pick	duck	bank
sick	truck	sulk
kick	silk	bunk
slick	milk	sank
trick	think	

Part C	
press	fuss
bliss	cross
dress	trace
grass	race
miss	face
class	force
glass	choice
pass	voice
bless	once
mess	fence
stress	since
hiss	dance
kiss	place
boss	ice
loss	nice
gloss	mice
moss	chance
toss	

Part D	
latch	blotch
match	clutch
catch	crutch
batch	reach
hatch	teach
patch	coach
fetch	speech
stretch	bench
sketch	drench
itch	inch
ditch	pinch
pitch	launch
stitch	bunch
witch	crunch
switch	arch
snatch	search
scratch	church
scotch	pouch
notch	touch

Test Charts

	Lesson 5	Lesson 10	Lesson 15	Lesson 20	Lesson 25	Lesson 30	30-Lesson Total
Super Speller	25	25	25	25	25	25	
	24	24	24	24	24	24	
	23	23	23	23	23	23	
Very Good Speller	22	22	22	22	22	22	**138 = Super Speller**
	21	21	21	21	21	21	
	20	20	20	20	20	20	
	19	19	19	19	19	19	
	18	18	18	18	18	18	
	17	17	17	17	17	17	
	16	16	16	16	16	16	
	15	15	15	15	15	15	
	14	14	14	14	14	14	
	13	13	13	13	13	13	
	12	12	12	12	12	12	
	11	11	11	11	11	11	
	10	10	10	10	10	10	
	9	9	9	9	9	9	
	8	8	8	8	8	8	
	7	7	7	7	7	7	
	6	6	6	6	6	6	
	5	5	5	5	5	5	
	4	4	4	4	4	4	
	3	3	3	3	3	3	
	2	2	2	2	2	2	
	1	1	1	1	1	1	

Test Charts

	Lesson 35	Lesson 40	Lesson 45	Lesson 50	Lesson 55	Lesson 60	30-Lesson Total
Super Speller	25	25	25	25	25	25	
	24	24	24	24	24	24	
	23	23	23	23	23	23	**138 = Super Speller**
Very Good Speller	22	22	22	22	22	22	
	21	21	21	21	21	21	
	20	20	20	20	20	20	
	19	19	19	19	19	19	
	18	18	18	18	18	18	
	17	17	17	17	17	17	
	16	16	16	16	16	16	
	15	15	15	15	15	15	
	14	14	14	14	14	14	
	13	13	13	13	13	13	
	12	12	12	12	12	12	
	11	11	11	11	11	11	
	10	10	10	10	10	10	
	9	9	9	9	9	9	
	8	8	8	8	8	8	
	7	7	7	7	7	7	
	6	6	6	6	6	6	
	5	5	5	5	5	5	
	4	4	4	4	4	4	
	3	3	3	3	3	3	
	2	2	2	2	2	2	
	1	1	1	1	1	1	

Test Charts

	Lesson 65	Lesson 70	Lesson 75	Lesson 80	Lesson 85	Lesson 90	30-Lesson Total
Super Speller	25	25	25	25	25	25	
	24	24	24	24	24	24	
	23	23	23	23	23	23	**138 = Super Speller**
Very Good Speller	22	22	22	22	22	22	
	21	21	21	21	21	21	
	20	20	20	20	20	20	
	19	19	19	19	19	19	
	18	18	18	18	18	18	
	17	17	17	17	17	17	
	16	16	16	16	16	16	
	15	15	15	15	15	15	
	14	14	14	14	14	14	
	13	13	13	13	13	13	
	12	12	12	12	12	12	
	11	11	11	11	11	11	
	10	10	10	10	10	10	
	9	9	9	9	9	9	
	8	8	8	8	8	8	
	7	7	7	7	7	7	
	6	6	6	6	6	6	
	5	5	5	5	5	5	
	4	4	4	4	4	4	
	3	3	3	3	3	3	
	2	2	2	2	2	2	
	1	1	1	1	1	1	

Test Charts

	Lesson 95	Lesson 100	Lesson 105	Lesson 110	Lesson 115	Lesson 120	30-Lesson Total
Super Speller	25	25	25	25	25	25	
	24	24	24	24	24	24	
	23	23	23	23	23	23	
Very Good Speller	22	22	22	22	22	22	**138 = Super Speller**
	21	21	21	21	21	21	
	20	20	20	20	20	20	
	19	19	19	19	19	19	
	18	18	18	18	18	18	
	17	17	17	17	17	17	
	16	16	16	16	16	16	
	15	15	15	15	15	15	
	14	14	14	14	14	14	
	13	13	13	13	13	13	
	12	12	12	12	12	12	
	11	11	11	11	11	11	
	10	10	10	10	10	10	
	9	9	9	9	9	9	
	8	8	8	8	8	8	
	7	7	7	7	7	7	
	6	6	6	6	6	6	
	5	5	5	5	5	5	
	4	4	4	4	4	4	
	3	3	3	3	3	3	
	2	2	2	2	2	2	
	1	1	1	1	1	1	